Constructive
Living

Constructive Living

David K. Reynolds

A Kolowalu Book
UNIVERSITY OF HAWAII PRESS
Honolulu

Manufactured in the United States of America
90 92 93 94 95 96   8 7 6 5

Library of Congress Cataloging in Publication Data

Reynolds, David K.
  Constructive living.

  (A Kolowalu book)
  Bibliography: p.
  1. Success. 2. Morita psychotherapy. I. Title.
BF637.S8R44   1984   158'.1   83–17868
ISBN 0–8248–0871–1

Contents

Preface

MORITA THERAPY, the basis of Constructive Living, isn't a "fun" therapy. It won't offer you new ways to play with your dreams and fantasies. It won't get you naked into a heated pool with a group of explorers of the psyche. It won't provide you with mystery or elaborate ritual or ready enlightenment.

But it will make solid sense to you, I think. It will slice through a lot of the excuses you've been feeding yourself (and others have been feeding you) for failing to live up to your potential. It will explain, and the explanations will check out with your experience. It will advise, and the advice will be down-to-earth, sound, practical. And it will leave totally up to you whether to act on the advice or not.

Some of you may find this lifeway too troublesome to bother with. Others may find a sort of salvation in it. All of you, I believe, will profit by considering it. Constructive Living presents a valuable alternative to *emotion*-centered living with all its ups and downs, all its uncontrollability. You will find there is a way to be *sure* of winning the game of everyday life.

It is perilous to write a book which argues that understanding is unimportant compared with doing. After all, most people read books in order to understand. It may go against your grain to be told that satisfying your hunger for knowledge *about* this way of life probably will have little impact on your life, but that trying some of the suggestions and exercises in this book (even without understanding fully *why* they work) may change your whole way of living. Nevertheless, I want you to check what you read here with your own experience.

The points I wish to make about Constructive Living are not especially valuable simply because I wrote them. They are valuable because they are the distilled wisdom of human beings in diverse cultures over hundreds of years. I am in no way remarkable. The most accurate thing that can be said about me is that I am "changeable." So are you. We aren't consistent in the way a character in a novel or a television serial is consistent. We are sometimes prejudiced, sometimes not; sometimes thoughtful, sometimes not; sometimes clever, sometimes not; sometimes suffering, sometimes not. From situation to situation, from minute to minute, and even within the same time period and place we have multiple identities that shift and flow in a complex dance of variation. There are no neurotics or geniuses or failures or fools. There are only neurotic moments, flashes of brilliance, failed opportunities, and stupid mistakes. But these moments, pleasant or unpleasant, can never fix us into rigid, immutable characters. We cannot help but change. This book is about choosing the direction of your changingness and acting upon your choice.

A number of people have contributed to this book. The Morita therapists and patients in Japan and the United States have taught me about Constructive Living. My student trainees have sharpened my understanding with their questions and critiques. Marguerite Reynolds and Eleanor Kwong typed the manuscript. My thanks to Elizabeth "Yuin" Hamilton for her assistance in compiling the list of Moritist maxims. Don Yoder contributed his sensitive copyediting of the manuscript, and Iris Wiley guided this work through the publication process with skill and encouragement. The ToDo Institute allowed the time for writing, reflection, and application of these principles. I am grateful to be riding on the efforts of these people.

Constructive Living

Introduction

THIS IS A BOOK about outgrowing your problems. Let us be clear at the outset that I cannot promise to make your problems go away. No one can. Life brings to all of us problems as well as successes, despair as well as joy. The Apostle Paul wrote that he had learned to adapt himself to every kind of circumstance, even being in jail. And the Buddha pointed out the inevitability of loss, sickness, aging, and death in human existence. Life cannot be an uninterrupted high. So if there are bound to be occasional lows it seems sensible to have a strategy for taking them in stride.

The same goes for shyness or chronic pain or tension or lethargy or any disability. If life has brought you such a problem (or even if you have created the problem yourself) you need to know how to take charge of it so that you can make the very best of what life allows. Anyone who promises more arouses my doubts about his or her ability to deliver.

The ideas behind this book have been around for hundreds of years. They are basically Buddhist, but don't let that fact mislead you. They are no more religious ideas than the concepts of psychoanalysis or the power of positive thinking or the principles of the American Constitution. They are simply the summed-up experiences of a lot of people who suffered themselves and treated other suffering people over the years. They make good common sense. Some eighty years ago a Japanese psychiatrist named Morita pulled together some of these ideas to turn his own life and the lives of many of his patients into demonstrations of the constructive possibilities that lie within us all. His methods are still practiced in Japan today. I have translated Morita's thought into terms understandable to Westerners and have added a notion of my own here and there, but the essence remains unchanged. The principles are as applicable to you and me as they were to the Japanese of Morita's day and the Japanese today. We are, after all, humans. And human suffering is human suffering wherever it is encountered.

Life Is Attention

RIGHT NOW lots of things are happening to you. Stimuli are flooding your senses. Your brain is even keeping track of what the big toe on your left foot is doing and how it is positioned, yet you probably weren't paying attention to that datum until you read about it just now. (Unless, of course, you recently broke that toe, in which case you've probably noticed it a lot more lately.) An astonishing amount of input is available, yet normally we're not overwhelmed by it. After all, a major function of our brain is to filter out masses of unnecessary data so that we can focus on essential information.

This observation leads us to an important point: Discomforting information is only discomforting when it gets through the filters of awareness and pops up in the middle of the spotlight of consciousness. In other words, we only hurt when we *notice* that we are hurting.

Surely you have heard of humans in battle or in accidents who performed tremendous feats while seriously injured, then collapsed later when the crisis was over and they *noticed* the damage and pain in their bodies. Perhaps you have read of the distraction caused by hypnosis or acupuncture needles that allows surgery to be carried out without anesthesia. A matter of attention. When you're not paying attention to your hurt you're not hurting. There may be tissue damage and bleeding, but you are not experiencing the pain; you aren't feeling it.

The same goes for thoughts. When you don't *focus* on your depressed thoughts and feelings, you're not depressed; so long as a compulsive handwasher is lost in watching a movie, his compulsion is no problem for him (it isn't even "there"); when a worried airplane passenger gets lost in the flavors and textures of her meal, she momentarily forgets her fear of flying.

This principle applies to pleasant as well as unpleasant feelings. The joy of purchasing a new car can disappear quickly when we suddenly note the salesman's discourtesy. Sexual feelings can evaporate when we notice some disturbing fault in a lover.

Awareness, awareness, awareness. That is where we live. That is all we know. That is life for each of us.

Some people try to hide from their anxieties, fears, anger, worries, and self-doubts by shifting their attention elsewhere. They use alcohol or drugs or positive thinking. They try to ignore and suppress their feelings. They take vacations, shift jobs, get divorced, or buy new clothes in order to redirect their attention away from some unpleasant incident or unhappy thoughts and feelings. Sometimes these tactics seem to pay off; sometimes they don't. Distraction alone isn't a solution to the torments of life.

This book offers a strategy for handling life's problems by both purposefully redirecting attention and engaging in constructive action—that is, *doing* something about the problem that caused the upset in the first place. The goal is not to ignore or suppress feelings, but to accept them as they happen to be at the moment . . . and then to get on with doing what is sensible and mature anyway. I cannot promise you that these ideas will make all your sorrows and impatience and insecurity disappear now and forever. No one can promise you endless bliss here on earth and then actually deliver. I can assure you, though, that if you put these principles into your daily life, you will feel somewhat better. Moreover, you will discover something much more important. You will discover that when your attention is fixed on behaving constructively your emotions won't be such a big deal to you. You'll find that in spite of how you happen to feel at the moment, you will be able to accomplish what you have set out to do—and that *accomplishment* is what really counts.

You see, the fully functioning human being isn't someone who is utterly free of pain and happy all the time. Not at all. The mature human being goes about doing what needs to be done regardless of whether that person feels great or terrible. Knowing that you are that kind of person with that kind of self-control brings all the satisfaction and confidence you will ever need. Even on days when the satisfaction and confidence just aren't there, you can get the job done anyway.

In the following pages we'll be learning how to outgrow our fears, not merely how to erase them temporarily. We'll emphasize positive self-development, not remedial therapy. We'll focus on the invigorating investigation of what needs doing out there in our world rather than stagnating in the pity pond of self-consciousness. We're headed in a new direction: investing *ourselves* in the world instead of wishing that others would save us. The study and practice aren't easy. You are more likely to give them a serious try after you've tried some easier paths and found that the effortless methods didn't work for you. The methods offered here do work, if you apply them to your life. They have to work, and so do you if you are to become the person you really want to be.

The major limitation of active expressive therapies in the West—the ones that attempt to get the patient to relive childhood traumas, to act out childhood impulses and desires—is that it is not "me-then" who is birth-screaming or shouting rage at my father or drinking unlimited malts. It is "me-now." And the "me-now" can't see or feel or think as the "me-then" did. My nervous system has changed, my body has grown, my understanding has developed. I possess only grown-up memories, edited memories, of what was "me-then."

The reality of the past cannot be changed. It may be fun to

play at being a child again. It may be useful sometimes to exert one's imagination and try to recreate what might have been long ago. But the past itself doesn't change.

We change only by changing the now. That is all we have to work with. What I *do* now is me and molds who I will become tomorrow. Make no mistake, there is no other time. The whole rests on what *I do now.*

What are you doing now? Well, you are reading. Your purpose may be to pass time, to avoid thinking about some troubling situation that faces you, to improve yourself, or even to prepare for an examination on the contents of this chapter. There are many possible reasons why you may be involved in this reading at this time. I suspect that you could come up with a variety of answers to the question "what is your purpose in reading this book?" depending on the mood you are in when questioned, who asks the question, how the query is put to you, and so forth.

At this point, though, I'm much less interested in exploring your purposes than in having you focus on the reality of what you are *doing*—that is, the fact that (for some reason) you are reading. The focus on *doing* is characteristic of Constructive Living. Rather than getting mixed up in a morass of motives, trying to analyze "why this reading now?", I want to zero in on the quality of this fact, this reading that is going on now. I want you to do the reading well. My goal at this moment is to help you to read well by writing in a way that will hold your attention. Because holding your attention is what I mean by reading well. Reading well, in other words, is being committed fully to the process of reading: to what you are *doing,* right now.

That's the ultimate goal of Constructive Living—to help you *do everything well,* with full attention. The more skill you develop in doing everything well, the more satisfaction and confidence you bring to your life. Whether you are reading, or carrying on a conversation, or making love, or playing tennis, or giving that speech in front of a group, you can be creating who you are and who you will become by *doing* the activity well, with full attention.

Now we all know that the first time we try to drive a car we're not very skillful. Driving proficiency comes after practice, after driving the car again and again. And confidence comes *after* we are skillful, after driving again and again.

So when I write that it is important always to do what we are doing "well," I don't mean doing it skillfully. Skill comes with practice. If this is the first time you've read a book like this, you may find certain ideas rough going. You can't say that you are skillful yet at reading this kind of material. When I say reading "well," I mean reading with full attention. It is the attention that turns practice into skill.

The fellow who idly hits at tennis balls while keeping his attention on the cute blonde strolling on the adjacent court isn't improving his tennis game even though he might tell you that he's practicing. Skill comes from practice with *attention* to what you are doing. This principle applies not only to tennis but to living itself. Constructive Living teaches you to pay attention to all of life's activities. You *practice* living moment by moment with all your attention. And you become skillful at living. That's the way to win in life—become skillful at it.

Life's Possibilities

NEARLY EVERYONE hopes. We dream about where we would like to be, what kind of place we would be living in, who would be nearby, what we would be doing, how we would be feeling. Our dreams develop and change but they provide more or less clear targets in life. Furthermore, we're all aware of obstacles between us and achieving those dreams. Often the major obstacle is ourselves. "I'd like to find the right person to share my life with, but I'm shy." "I could really advance in the office if I were just more aggressive." "I'm too pushy; I scare people off." "Why couldn't I have been born beautiful (or rich or smart or a member of another race)?" "I'm so tense all the time I can't get anything done." "I lack confidence." "I need more formal education." "Why do I keep on messing up my life this way?"

Common Sense About Feelings

Each of us is aware, painfully aware, of some of the ways we keep ourselves from being who we want to be. This book offers an overall strategy for achieving what is possible in life for you. It suggests ways of using your energy and attention sensibly without wasting your resources on trying to do the impossible.

What do I mean "trying to do the impossible"? Well, for one thing, you can't *make* yourself feel good; no one can. When you are feeling sad or lonely or worried or embarrassed or generally beaten down by life, you can't sit down and simply will yourself to feel happy and confident and eager to take on the world. To try to make yourself feel what you're not feeling is foolishness. The power of positive thinking is bunk if it pretends to see joy where there is no joy or hope when you feel hopeless. Now if I can't make myself feel good by an effort of will, I certainly can't make anybody else feel good, either, by wishing it were so.

The first principle I want you to learn is a tough one, but I think you'll find it true enough when you check it against your own experience. The principle is: *Feelings are uncontrollable directly by the will.* You can't make yourself feel anything. Now there are ways you can indirectly influence your anxiety or anger or any other emotion, and we're coming to them shortly. But we've got to start with the hard reality that we can't think ourselves into a constant state of bliss. To try to do so is a waste of time. It's probably for the best anyway (as we will see), since the effort just distracts us from working on what is realistically changeable and controllable: our behavior. But more of that later.

Already there is some benefit from recognizing that feelings aren't controllable. If we can't control them, we certainly can't be held responsible for them. This means that any feeling—seething hatred, erotic urges, grudges, disappointment, timidity, grouchiness, lethargy—is "all right" in the sense that you're not morally responsible for it. You're not a Bad Person for having the emotion. You may prefer some feelings to others, but you're not "wrong" for feeling something. It's not necessary to feel guilty about feeling depressed. Of course, if you do feel guilty about feeling depressed, that's all right. You don't have to feel guilty about feeling guilty about feeling depressed. But if you do, you do. And that leads to the second principle: *Feelings must be recognized and accepted as they are.*

Let's be realistic. If you can't control your feelings directly by willpower, and you aren't responsible for what you're feeling, the best strategy for dealing with feelings is to accept them and see what you can learn from them. Sometimes feelings give us signals about something we need to do. If I feel nervous before a lecture, I'm prompted to spend time preparing the speech. If you suddenly start feeling uncomfortable every time your supervisors are around, you may need to talk things over with them. The notion I'm trying to get across here is simply this: Feelings often arise out of situations that can be changed. And then the feelings too will change.

The third principle is closely related to the second: *Every feeling, however unpleasant, has its uses.* Pain returns us to the here and now; guilt causes us to reexamine our purposes; grief prompts reevaluations and a change in behavior; anxiety leads to care and preparation; fear mobilizes our bodies for action. Certainly anyone can be blown about by these discomforting feelings. They don't *necessarily* provoke positive changes. Nevertheless, even within the most unpleasant emotions there is potential for good. They can be used.

Recognizing this potential benefit leads us to treasure all feelings. Rather than trying vainly to get rid of some of them, we should be trying to learn from all of them. Recognizing the uses of guilt, for example, also points out the folly of therapies that aim at removing guilt feelings (or anxieties or fears or grief). Such therapeutic goals are rather like trying to remove the body's immune system because allergies are bothersome.

To be sure we would all prefer to learn from pleasant emotions rather than unpleasant ones. Fortunately, there are in fact ways of influencing our emotions, but before we get to that strategy we need to consider the fourth principle: *Feelings fade in time unless they are restimulated.* Given time the worst grief, pain, shock, or fright will lose its edge and become little more than a memory. Childbirth, the dentist's drill, the loss of a loved one, the sideache, the rage during that argument—all fade unless something happens to stir up those feelings again. And herein lies hope for the depressed, the embarrassed, the disconsolate: These feelings won't maintain this intensity forever. They, too, shall pass away.

What may seem less gratifying is the observation that this principle applies to pleasant feelings as well as to unpleasant ones. My joy won't last either, nor will my contentment, nor love, nor peace of mind. These feelings, too, fade . . . unless they are restimulated.

What causes the vast wave of feeling to splash over our psyches again? Certainly another quarrel can call forth faded resentment and anger, another loss can rekindle feelings of abandonment, a movie can reenergize buried feelings of love and tenderness, and a surprise package can revitalize feelings of being loved and joy. Passively waiting for events to reexcite good feelings and disagreeable passions is much too fatalistic, however. There is a way we can *actively* involve ourselves in affecting our emotions.

The fifth principle is: *Feelings can be indirectly influenced by behavior.* You can use your behavior to beckon desirable feelings and reduce the influence of undesirable ones. Here is the handle on our moods that life has supplied. Note that the term "influenced" is used in the fifth principle and not the term "controlled." No matter what we do, certain strong feelings are intransigent and must, in keeping with principle four, be waited out until they fade. Still, some influence is better than none at all. How does the principle work?

Jennifer is nearly twenty. Several weeks ago her boyfriend dumped her for a pert redhead he described as "easier and more fun." Jennifer sits on her bed playing records that Jeff used to like, looking at a snapshot of him, replaying in her mind the good times they had together, and crying her heart out. Jennifer is actively involved in keeping her sorrow going. She is doing things that restimulate feelings of loss and injustice. A friend of Jeff's has been waiting in the wings for this opportunity, but when he calls Jennifer tells him she doesn't feel like going out now. Poor Jennifer! Poor ignorant Jennifer! Her love for Jeff would fade like any other sentiment if only her behavior would give it a chance.

Sue feels terrible about being fat. The solution to her ugly feelings about herself is simple. She needs to eat less and exercise more. But she isn't often in the mood for exercise, she complains; and besides, she enjoys eating. Put another way, Sue lets her feelings control her behavior and the result is guilt and embarrassment about her size. In order to produce some positive change, the place to enter Sue's corkscrew of corpulence is at the point of behavior. While accepting the reality that she doesn't enjoy exercising and does enjoy eating, Sue must increase the exercise and decrease the gluttony. It's as simple (and as hard) as that.

Hal is frustrated about studying. Maxine says she would like to give up smoking. Art worries about his shyness. Kathy is at odds with her mother all the time. Corinne gets bored and can't hold a job. Their problems are all different yet all the same. They struggle with themselves in an exhausting nonproductive way because they don't recognize the five principles of feelings. Those principles are nothing more than common-sense observations of how feelings affect us and how our behavior affects feelings. Once we fully understand them we are on the way to sensible control over our lives.

Taking Charge of Behavior

What you are about to read concerning behavior is neither mysterious nor inscrutably Oriental. Yet it is part of a system of thought and action developed by a Japanese psychiatry professor named Morita some eighty years ago. He understood himself and his patients very well. Check out his insights on your own behavior. I think you will find a marvelous correspondence.

America is a land of freedom, we say. Yet all around us are

restrictions on what we can do. Only designated persons can prescribe medicine, only certain drugs can be taken legally, streets should be crossed only when the traffic light is green, children under a certain age cannot work for wages, it is impolite to sneeze in someone's face, social greetings are required at parties, we are expected to speak on one level of formality to our bosses and another way to our friends. We are not entirely free in what we do, of course. And no one really wants to live an absolutely unfettered life. Children who are given too much leeway are miserable; they actually seek limits and direction from adults. Mentally disturbed people also seem more comfortable when a warm but firm hand limits the boundaries of their "crazy" behavior. Even artists are never truly free. They voluntarily take on the limits of the medium they use, the style they employ, the model, the patron, time constraints, the question of cost, and so on.

We are able to operate within these limits, even to enjoy some of them, because our behavior is controllable in a way that our feelings are not. There is a very special satisfaction for the Artist of Living who works within life's limits to produce a fine self-portrait. The more control we develop over our actions, the more chance we have of producing a self we can be proud of.

More than one science fiction story has been built around the idea of someone traveling in time and making some minute change in the past—emerging from the time machine, for example, and stepping on an ant—and then returning to find the present greatly altered by the rippling effects of that trivial act. One implication of such tales is that no act is trivial. *Everything* we do changes the future in one way or another. We are all time travelers.

Let me state the next principle flatly: *We are responsible for what we do no matter how we feel at the time.* How often have you heard people use their feelings as an excuse for behaving irresponsibly? "I didn't do the homework because I just didn't feel like it." "I couldn't ask her to have dinner with me because I'm shy." "I shot him because I was angry." "I won't eat because I'm resentful." "I stayed in the house for months because of my grief." "I can't drive on a freeway because I'm scared." Each of these statements contains two segments: one about behavior and one about feelings. I can't, I won't, I didn't . . . *because* I feel, I felt.

We have already seen that emotions are not directly controllable by the will. We can't make ourselves feel something directly by wishing the change. Nevertheless, no matter what the feelings, we can control our *actions* if we choose to exert ourselves. A lot of people find it easier to give in and let their feelings control their behavior much of the time. That course always leads, eventually, to misery and failure. Let's be realistic. Although it sounds romantic to "go with the flow" of impulses and emotions, the end result will be some bills unpaid, some deadlines unmet, some social responsibilities unfulfilled. Allowing yourself to be dominated by shifting emotions will result in the loss of your job, separation from dependable friends, blows to your self-esteem, poor health, and pretty severe restrictions on your freedom to move around. (You'll get locked up, beat up, maybe killed.) Reality keeps demanding self-controlled behavior.

All this may sound rather grim so far. We have to maintain control in order to survive and succeed. But where is the spontaneity? Where is the joy of living? We aren't robots, after all. We don't want simply to go around paying bills, showing up daily for work, meeting our social debts, holding ourselves back from slugging the impolite bus driver. Surely there is more to life than that.

Yet it is precisely our ability to manage our behavior that opens the door to a rich emotional life. Some people who haven't got their conduct under control are afraid of their feelings. They are worried that if they allow their passions to well up they are going to behave themselves into a lot of trouble. So they try to sit on their feelings; they try to ignore them; they try not to feel. Such people usually come in for therapy complaining that life is gray and meaningless.

For these clients it is necessary to begin by restoring some order to their disarrayed lives. Beginning with simple activities—preparing three meals a day, instituting an exercise program, ensuring sufficient hours in bed—they must move toward regaining control over their behavior. These patients are advised that sometimes they won't feel like exercising or preparing a meal, yet they are to do these tasks anyway during this training period. As the self-discipline of behavior progresses, bigger emotional roadblocks emerge. These impulses and moods, too, are to be accepted without struggle while the constructive action continues.

And what is the result? They become free to recognize and feel the *whole* range of emotions because they know that their actions are properly managed. I can feel the depths of anger because I'm confident that I won't stupidly lash out at someone. I can fall into infatuated love again and again because nothing embarrassing or foolish will result. And so on. Behavioral responsibility grants me permission to feel. There is an old saying that temptation is understood fully only by the person who resists it repeatedly. Certainly, resisting our passions gives us a special perspective on them that the emotional glutton can never achieve.

There is another sense in which behavior is linked to feeling. Not only does tamed behavior allow spirited feeling, but often behavior can be used indirectly to generate the sorts of feelings you desire. You can create a hyped-up feeling by dancing, running, sports, listening to certain kinds of music, viewing flashing colors, conversing with a provocative companion, and so forth. Similarly, you can deliberately foster a calmer, peaceful state of mind—by sitting quietly, turning down the music, meditating, lowering the lights, lying still for a gentle massage, and the like. Anger, love, desire, confidence, and many other states of mind can be created daily by these means. The notion here is that we can make rational use of behavior to bring about desired moods and tempers.

There is yet another way that mastering our behavior can result in positive feelings. My experience is, and most likely yours is no different, that life has brought its greatest rewards when I have accomplished some goal in spite of distractions from within and without. When a book is published, when a marriage is consummated, when a long-awaited trip is taken, when a degree is earned, when a business deal succeeds, when children mature and set their own course as young adults, when a patient improves—each of these situations involves the culmination of planning and effort. One pauses and reflects upon what has been accomplished. To be sure, a successful outcome depends on a complex of circumstances and outside support. Yet to see one's own effort as a key to the event is satisfying in proportion to the behavior invested. The tomatoes that you have planted, watered, protected, and picked have special meaning whatever their size and shape. For all my dreams, I am what I do.

Self-Centeredness
and Suffering

THE MOST PEACEFUL people I know have given themselves away. One is a Buddhist nun living in a temple community in rural Japan without a newspaper, radio, or television. This tiny woman looks twenty years younger than her true age. After much suffering during a personal crisis she came to live in this temple where she spends a great deal of time listening to others' outpourings of grief and confession. After years of service without any income she was sent into town with fifty dollars to buy something for herself. She returned to the temple with the same fifty dollars having found nothing she wanted or needed. She seems to know what is important.

Another acquaintance of mine is a black woman with a couple of children and a houseful of male psychiatric patients. In her boarding house, an aftercare facility for the mentally disturbed, she pauses at night by each closed bedroom door to pray for the improvement of her wards. She even took them on her vacation to Hawaii. An amazing woman!

These women have found a secret of life: Satisfaction comes from abandoning the self. Certainly they have moments of misery, times of sickness and grief, periods of doubt and worry. But soon they are back again at the business of adding to the lives of others. Then they sparkle.

Hurting Ourselves

On the other hand, the most miserable people I have known have been self-focused. They worry about getting *their* share;

they evaluate everyone's acts in terms of how they themselves are affected. They are all wrapped up in themselves and the wrapping has a mirror finish.

Take the case of a young fellow I worked with in Japan. He was an ordinary looking fellow who behaved himself in an ordinary way in public. Yet whenever he went shopping or riding a train, he felt as if people were staring at him—perhaps they were mocking him, he said. I rode the train with him and we shopped together to see whether I sensed this strange notoriety, too. It all seemed to be in his imagination. Part of the problem stemmed from an unsatisfying and even cruel homosexual relationship in which the young man was involved. He felt guilty about it, but he was unwilling to give it up. This quandary turned his attention inward to the degree that in his mind nearly everyone seemed to be noticing him in the same way that he was focusing on himself. Everything became self-referred. Within months of severing the homosexual relationship his condition improved notably. The moral of this tale is not that homosexuality will drive you crazy, of course, but rather that an exclusive self-focus will drive you miserable.

Some people try to cheat life in this way. They think that if the path of self-sacrifice leads to happiness, they will pretend to give themselves to other people through volunteer work or charity or church activities. Their true purpose, though, is to make themselves as happy as possible. So they keep checking themselves. Am I happier now than before? There's a football game on television this morning. Would I be happier watching it or participating in the service activity planned for this morning? How's my progress so far? They keep referring their attention back to their own desires. The whole notion of self-loss through service is betrayed.

To be sure, giving up the self is a relative thing. Clearly we must continue to eat or otherwise protect and nourish ourselves. The Buddhist nun I spoke of fully enjoys her meals. She eats with zest, sleeps soundly, exercises by working in the temple fields and gardens. The eating, sleeping, and exercising are enjoyable, but they are also part of the whole picture of service—part of the preparation for offering a listening ear and guidance to others.

The Japanese language offers unique insights into human psychology. There are words in Japanese for emotions that I suppose all humans feel at one time or another but have no equivalent labels in English. *"Sumanai,"* for example, sometimes refers to a feeling you get when receiving a present you don't deserve—a mixture of gratitude, respect for the giver, shame that you're not really worthy of the gift, elation for getting it anyway, and so forth. The Japanese language uses a single word for self-centered and selfish. The word is *"jiko-chūshin."* It means, literally, the self in the middle of the heart—the ego in the center of the mind. It means putting Old Number One first.

I was crossing the street with an acquaintance of mine one day when some papers blew out of a passing car. The car stopped and several students jumped out to collect the scattered sheets. My impulse was to run and help them. Traffic stopped; others rushed to their aid; but my acquaintance just kept on walking. If he noticed it at all, he didn't care about their papers. He was all wrapped up in himself. That fellow was perhaps the most miserable person I've ever known. He was so unsatisfied with his life, in fact, that he made several serious attempts at killing himself: pills, suffocation, even a gunshot wound near his heart.

Some people would say that this young man needs to straighten out his thinking and feelings before he will be motivated to help those students pick up their flying papers. I don't think he has time to do that—more than ten years of conventional therapy haven't helped appreciably. Furthermore, I don't think trying to straighten out feelings first is a sensible or even realistic course. My guess is that picking up the papers will help develop the *other*-centeredness that my young friend needs. The *doing* changes the attitudes. The service alters the suffering self.

Before you get the notion that I'm merely a simpleminded do-gooder, let me make it clear that I see serving others as part of a larger panorama of cutting down on self-centeredness. The goal of Constructive Living is not merely noticing what others need but noticing the requirements of the situations that reality presents to us moment by moment. If we are distracted by our own nervousness and desires we don't attend to what is happening in our immediate world.

Let me offer another example. My office is located in a security building. When my clients arrive I come to the foyer to escort them up a flight of stairs, down a corridor, and up a second flight to the door of the office. Recently one of my clients said that she considered her knowledge of Morita Therapy to be pretty complete after only five sessions. At the end of the hour I asked her to lead me back to the foyer by the route we had taken earlier. Not only had we used the same route for five sessions, but twice before I had asked her to lead me back to the foyer and front door. On those previous occasions, and this time too, she was unable to find the simple route downstairs. She hadn't *noticed* where she was going—because of her self-focus, her anxiety, her habit of leaving things to the direction of authority figures, or whatever. The point is that she was not attending to the reality of the situation even after five sessions. Clearly her experiential understanding of Constructive Living didn't match her intellectual understanding.

I used to tell my students that people who suffer neurotically —that is, people who are obsessed with their suffering—have the potential for becoming not only nonneurotic but better than normal. The more I read of Morita's writings and the more experience I accumulate with my students and clients, the more it becomes clear that the connection between suffering and superiority is even stronger than that. Neurotic obsessed suffering is *essential* for greatness. Morita pointed out that the Buddha, Shinran, and Hakuin—three of the religious leaders most respected by the Japanese—all felt tormented by the human condition before they broke through to their universal insights.

Why should this relationship hold? Part of the answer lies in the fact that our mental agony is one aspect of reality for us. We cannot hide in theories and abstractions when we are hurting. We are forced to face this aspect of reality again and again. The way we come to handle our suffering sets a pattern for the way we deal with other aspects of reality. That reality of pain will rise into our awareness again and again to test the measure of our life solutions. As Morita put it: "Self-development doesn't aim to make life easy. It aims at making efforts to succeed even when we're failing."

On Being "Realistic"

In most books, a chapter on the nature of reality would involve a tough philosophical discourse. Morita, however, insisted that we could all pretty much agree on his meaning in this case. "That flower is red, that willow is green—to understand such things is not difficult at all."

Morita saw that his approach to Constructive Living was so radical that it could be compared to the Copernican revolution. In fact, he used that very analogy. Taking his metaphor a step further, we can say that although the neurotic's subjective world seems to have the *self* at center, in fact the neurotic himself revolves about reality but refuses to acknowledge it!

What is this reality around which everyone's life turns? It is the reality that you weigh so many pounds, that you can't put your hand through a closed door, that grass is green, that some-one doesn't like you, that you haven't the size or charm or intel-ligence you might wish for, that your body bleeds when cut, that someday you will die. Simply pointing to elements of real-ity in this way will not satisfy philosophers, in all probability, yet I write only of the common everyday reality we know to exist.

The problem with all of us at one time or another is this: When we ignore the fact that reality acts on us in an orderly, understandable way, we begin thinking in very unrealistic ways. The mother who spends her whole day worrying about what might happen to her beloved daughter at school, the young man so enraptured with his vision of the latest film starlet that he gets nothing done at work, the teenager who believes that if only his nose were smaller (if only her pimples were gone) then life would be trouble free—such people are living in worlds of unreality. They have distracted themselves from the truth of the dusty floors, the desk piled high with papers, the unwritten his-tory lesson.

The first step in changing reality is to recognize it as it is *now*. There is no need to wish it were otherwise. It simply is. Pleasant or not, it is. Then comes behavior that acts on the present real-ity. Behavior can change what is. We may have visions of what will be. We cannot (and need not) prevent these dreams. But the visions won't change the future. Action—in the present—changes the future. A trip of ten thousand miles starts out with one step, not with a fantasy about travel.

"If you are confronted by a path with a thousand branches," says Morita, "you have no option but to try them one by one." Standing at the crossroad imagining the possible end point of each path takes us nowhere beyond the crossroad. Choosing one of the paths, we walk along discovering its distant bounda-ries and terminations, choosing again and again among its branches. It is the action of walking that shows us where the path leads.

Finding the Kernel of Good

In the late 1960s when I began conducting research in Japan, I had rigid notions about how to set up interviews, gather data, and interpret what I saw. Occasionally a Japanese advisor would suggest that a plan was ill-conceived—another course might be better—but I usually pursued my original plan. Those who offered their advice seemed not at all rattled when I stubbornly refused to try their alternative courses. They let me go ahead and bang myself against some barrier until I came around to trying the Japanese way of tackling the problem. And they never followed up with a smug "I told you so."

One reason why they could allow their advice to be ignored without personal affront was that they could see the good in my way of trying, in my stubbornness, in my making mistakes. Their inclination was to search for wisdom in my sentences of broken Japanese and to assume that when they couldn't find much sense it was their own error in interpretation and not my simplemindedness or triviality. In other words they looked for the good in my motives and acts. This habit of searching for the good applied not only to my case but to everyone. The Japanese people are skillful at excusing faults in themselves and others as they focus on the positive elements of some deed.

Americans, I think, are more critical. Certainly, though we say that we are independent and freedom loving, we Americans seem often to put obedience before independence. The nurse in an American hospital who finds a patient walking in the corridor when he should be confined to bed is likely to respond with alarm that the doctor's orders are being violated. Her reaction is apt to be self-protective concern as well as concern for the misbehaving patient. Her counterpart in Japan is less likely to respond directly to the rule violation and much more likely to consider the needs of the patient that would prompt his leaving bed.

Taoism suggests that no one ever tells a lie. Of course people lie, I used to think. What, I wondered, could be the meaning of such a patently false statement? In time I realized one interpretation: If we understand the meaning behind what appears to be a lie, we find truth. The little boy with his hand in the cookie jar and crumbs on his shirt denies that he ate any cookies. "I didn't eat any" really means "I don't want to be scolded for what I did." Listening with the third ear can be a kind of listening for the truth underlying a statement. Taoism's cousin, Buddhism, teaches that humans are basically good, only misdirected or miseducated. If we truly understood the consequences of our acts, the Buddhist holds, we would all act morally and constructively all of the time.

What has all this to do with the strategy of living outlined in this book? The point is that in every stressful situation, in every neurotic symptom, in every misdeed, there are elements of good. I try not to focus on the faults of my clients but on the distorted purity that underlies their problems. Consider the client who is sure she has heart disease although repeated medical examinations are all consistently negative. Finally someone tells her the problem is psychological and refers her to our center for counseling. She says that she shouldn't have these fears about heart disease. She knows she should trust medical opinion. But her father died of a heart attack at fifty-six years of age, and soon my client, too, will be fifty-six. After listening to her story, I point out that her fear of heart disease is a very good thing. I, too, am afraid of heart disease. Anyone who is not afraid of this dreadful disease is unusual. Being afraid prompts us to get checkups, to watch what we eat, to watch how we live.

There is nothing wrong with a fear of illness (or public speaking or examinations or parties or flying). This woman's problem was that she allowed her anxiety to interfere with her responsibilities as homemaker and citizen and neighbor. She had recently begun preparing meals irregularly, for example, causing disruption and arguments in her family. The sensible fear of a heart attack had been allowed to intrude on her daily life. And the more she tried to erase the fear, the more guilt she felt about being phobic. The more she wished she were different, the more she found her attention pulled toward herself and the normal aches and fatigue that she interpreted as incipient malfunctioning of her heart. The good became misdirected. The solution was education, acceptance, and a change in behavior. When she stopped struggling and focused her attention on carrying her share of the world's work and play, the fears diminished. They faded from forefront to background.

Grief carries kernels of good. Physical pain does, too, as we will see shortly. Shyness grows out of the natural desire to be liked and respected. A change at work or home often brings increased sensitivity and alertness that may be misdirected into anxiety and worry. But the good, the plus, the positive is there too. I am not promoting Pollyanna's Position: that everything works out for the best in this best of all possible worlds. No amount of looking on the bright side will revive a dead child, return our youth, cure an alcoholic, or give someone confidence. Nevertheless, for every disaster some meaning can be constructed. Within every worry is an opportunity for positive action. In every lie there is a kernel of truth. Behind every neurotic symptom is the misdirected desire to live fully and well.

What to Do About
Life's Rough Times

LIFE BRINGS US a variety of curves and passing lanes, detours and stop signs, freeways, and chuck holes, and green lights, and flat tires. Failure or fear of the possibility of failure plague many people who want so much to do well in life. Shyness, too, particularly among some young people seems to be a major roadblock interfering with their reaching life's destinations. Depression, grief, fear, stress, physical ailments, and troubled social relationships seem to flash warning lights in everyone's life at one time or another. In this chapter we shall consider how to handle some of the common road hazards of living using the principles of Constructive Living.

Failure

Life isn't fair, wrote Robert Heinlein. I certainly agree. At least in no simple sense do I see people consistently getting what they deserve. "The rain falls on the just and on the unjust." That's the way it is. Sometimes we try hard, put forth our best effort, and fail. Sometimes life plops a ripe fruit in our laps as we lounge in the sunshine. Unpredictable. We can act to improve the odds of achieving success, but nothing guarantees it.

Some people get discouraged soon after giving Constructive Living a try. They say they focused on getting things done in their lives and they started feeling better right away. But after a while there seemed to be even more that needed doing. And some mornings they woke up feeling terrible even though they were doing their level best. And furthermore, although they were paying more attention to work at the office or at home, things were going badly. Their spouses were still angry. No one was responding to the ads they placed or the job applications they filed so diligently. It just wasn't fair.

They had missed the point of Constructive Living. No one can guarantee pain-free living. No one can guarantee that success will follow our best effort. Our chances of success do improve as we behave responsibly, but sometimes we'll fail anyway. That's all right. Failure presents something else for us to do, just as success does. It's in the responding to every moment's needs, regardless of success or failure, that we mature. Morita said that self-development doesn't mean making life easy; it means making efforts to succeed even while we are failing. That makes sense.

Let me offer an example. I'm driving down the Santa Monica freeway heading for an appointment at the Marina. My right rear tire blows out. Oh no! Well, what needs to be done now? I pull over to the shoulder and open the trunk to get at the spare. Uh oh! The spare is flat. What needs doing now? I start looking for a call box to phone the Auto Club. Up pulls a Highway Patrol car. My car isn't far enough onto the shoulder. The officer would like to see my driver's license. I discover that my wallet is in the briefcase at home. Oh, my! What needs to be done now? This story could go on and on. If the focus is on evaluating what is happening to me, I'm involved in a losing game—flat tire, bad spare, traffic ticket, no license at hand, late for an appointment, and so forth. If the focus is on finding the best response to the circumstances, then I'm back in a game with possibilities of winning. I do what I can do. Responding intelligently will probably change the situation for the better, but it will surely change me. Constructive Living is working on what's out there that needs doing, but it is also working on building a certain kind of me.

So if you become discouraged somewhere along the way while giving Constructive Living an experiential try, I have a suggestion. Simply note that you are discouraged and remember that being discouraged is a feeling. That's interesting; I'm discouraged. Already you have some distance from your discouragement. Next resolve to accept that feeling as it is and not waste time struggling with it directly. It's all right (though unpleasant) to be discouraged. Next try to figure out what's causing the feeling and what the feeling is signaling you to do about your present reality. In other words, there may be something that needs doing in your world that you *can* do. And one result of the doing might be that the discouragement will go away. Don't, repeat, don't take action in order to get rid of the discouragement. Take action to change what needs changing. Take action to respond to your situation. Let the discouragement take care of itself.

Sometimes no matter what you do there is no immediate relief from the disappointment. In that case you must simply accept the discouragement and go about your business. The feelings will pass. The sooner your attention shifts to responsible behavior, the sooner your feelings will fade.

Remember to begin by recognizing feelings pleasant or unpleasant. Don't begin by ignoring or denying them. See whether they have a message for you about some action you need to take. Then behave responsibly. If the feeling remains, is there something else you need to do? If not, go on about living without excessive interest in the feeling. There is something much bigger at stake here than the momentary discomfort of regret and discouragement. You are constructing a finer, deeper, stronger you.

As you engage in an organized program of Constructive Living, there will probably be rapid relief from some of your problems. You will find yourself with more energy, more time, and higher spirits . . . for a while. That honeymoon period will probably fade within a few weeks. As the novelty wears off and it gets harder to put forth the effort, hour by hour, in maintaining the program, you'll begin to find excuses for drifting back to old habits. After all, you will be feeling better. Maybe you don't need the program of Constructive Living any more.

Beware! This trap should alert you that your purpose has been to feel better and not to overcome your feelings. Back to old habits of careless behavior and unclear purpose, you'll eventually start feeling depressed and troubled again. Don't give up. Start again on constructive behavior. But this time truly accept whatever feelings may come and cling to your purpose. Although you may not understand how or why these principles work, you cannot help recognizing their impact on your life as you apply them with diligence.

Shyness

There are many kinds of shyness. Jim has trouble meeting women. He blushes and stammers whenever he tries to approach an attractive lady. He has no trouble conversing with his sister, his female coworkers at the office, or homely women. But whenever he comes across someone who appeals to him he avoids her. In the back of his mind, though, he hopes that she'll somehow notice him and initiate something.

Helen says she's afraid of boys. She is twenty-two and feeling pressure from her family to marry and raise a family. Helen sees herself as ugly and clumsy and certainly not built as well as she'd like to be. I suspect that most people would find her self-criticism far too harsh. Helen once had a "bad experience" with a man who seemed bent on satisfying his own needs through the use of Helen's admiration and body. She knows all men aren't like that, but she still says no even when she wants to go out. Then she kicks herself for refusing the invitation.

Dan does well with the women in his life. His problem is the trouble he has asserting himself when his boss, minister, or professor is around. Dan is going back to college at his company's expense. Sometimes what the professor says in class is contrary to Dan's experience in engineering over the past ten years. He wants to speak up, to question, but he wonders whether he would just make a fool of himself in front of everybody and, moreover, get the professor mad at him. While he sits there wondering, the lecture moves ahead and it's too late to interrupt. Dan has a similar problem when it comes to asking for a raise or promotion. His record shows real success, yet he seems to be passed over again and again as his fellow workers climb up the corporate hierarchy.

Eva can't meet other people's eyes while talking with them. John worries that his breath offends people. Harry gets so nervous at a party that his stomach starts churning out gas. Karilee's hands tremble as she serves dinner to her husband's business guests. Wanda believes people stare at her on the bus. Corinne hasn't left her home for nearly a year because she's afraid of meeting people outside where the streets aren't safe. Tim likes his in-laws but avoids them for no apparent reason except that he feels "uncomfortable" around them. In the midst of his first pelvic exam, Ramon suddenly realizes that his patient is also an attractive young lady. He gets flustered and wonders whether he truly belongs in medical school. Marlene looks out over the faces of her audience and freezes.

Whether or not all these examples strictly belong in a category labelled "shyness," they all involve discomfort around others. These people are very much aware of the liability their shyness has become. They want to change but feel that they can't. They compare themselves with others around them, others who appear supremely confident and socially skilled, and they feel even worse. What's wrong with me? Why can't I be like other people? Why do I have this block in my life?

Most of my American clients are surprised to learn that their problems are not uncommon at all. In fact, they are shared by Japanese patients as well. The Japanese seem better at hiding their liabilities from others though, at putting on a good front. In Japan the client usually feels that he is the only one suffering from his form of shyness; in America the client is more likely to suspect that his anxieties are shared by others, but not many. In both cultures, clients are relieved to learn that their misery is not only seen frequently but also pretty well understood. Success rates of Morita's method of Constructive Living in terms of cured and improved clients are up in the ninety percent range according to studies from Japan. Not bad, nine out of ten.

So what's the secret of overcoming shyness? The first step is recognizing the reality that you're shy and accepting it. Well, recognition is no problem. The world keeps beating me over the head with information confirming that fact. I'm shy. Yes, me too! Me, author of books, guest speaker on the chicken-a-la-king circuit, university professor, world traveler—shy. I'm the guy whose shirt is drenched with perspiration after a lecture, whose palms are clammy as I shake hands with the dean of the school, who sometimes avoids and rarely enjoys cocktail parties. Recognition was no problem for me. Acceptance took a little longer.

You see, a lot of a shy person's attention gets wasted on wishing he weren't the way he is. He focuses just on this aspect of himself, how it hampers his life, wondering whether other people notice his shyness. He may have plenty of other fine qualities, but he's like the person who got ninety out of a hundred on a test and thinks only about the ten points he missed. Some shy people go beyond wishing they were different and try to make themselves not shy. One method that doesn't really work is to put on a false front and pretend to yourself and others you're not the way you are. Another method that rarely works is to spend a lot of time in introspection trying to remember past events that may have contributed to your shyness—the time your father died, the time you were turned down for a prom, the embarrassment of your uncle's alcoholism, the new classmates you had to face each time your family moved. There is a more reliable way, though, to overcome the chains of shyness. It is to be shy.

What do I mean? I mean that if you are uncomfortable around people of the opposite sex, then you are uncomfortable. That's reality. *Never deny reality.* To pretend, to ignore, to wish never changes anything. While accepting the reality of your shyness, go on doing what you need to do in life. That means in spite of quivering knees and pounding heart, call that guy or gal you'd like to know better, tell your boss you'd do better work if he didn't stand at your shoulder all the time, make that speech, do the shopping in that crowded store. Call, tell, make, do— those are all actions. Get on about living even though you are shy. Paradoxically, the more you do these things, the less shy you will feel. Not only will you become more skillful and confident in social situations by gaining experience in them (no one ever became a good golfer just by watching) but you will be turning more and more attention away from yourself (and your own problems) toward the reality out there.

I marvel at the way each of my clients sees his own predicament as deadly serious while regarding shyness in others as trivial and sometimes even amusing. The man who is afraid to speak in public can't understand how anyone could be upset just by shopping in a crowded department store. The woman who's afraid to go out with young men can't see why someone would be shy around his boss. The man who sees himself as ugly or smelly or clumsy can't imagine how a pretty, fragrant, graceful girl could ever lack confidence when dealing with others. Our own plight can blind us to what the world (and the people in it) are really like.

Shyness isn't like a blemish. It isn't something that can be neatly excised by some mystical mental surgery. Shyness is a

point of view. Shyness *is* me sometimes. It fills my awareness.
More and more I've learned to recognize that creeping self-consciousness, the worry about what others are thinking of me, the
wishing that they would like me, and so forth—to recognize it
and say to myself something like "Hmmmm, isn't that interesting. Here comes shyness again. Now what needs to be done?"
At that point my attention shifts from me to the *situation* in
which I find myself. I greet someone, try to find out something
about their values and experiences; I stop rambling and get to
the point of the telephone conversation; I prod the client to put
more effort into practicing the therapeutic principles; I look at
my notes and proceed with the lecture; I do what needs doing.
And the self-consciousness disappears.

But be careful here. I don't shift my attention to the situation
at hand *in order to* get rid of this self-consciousness. That is not
my purpose at all. I continue with the lecture because there is a
lecture going on and it needs to be completed. I prod the client
because that is part of my responsibility as his guide. The situation requires these actions from me. The momentary self-focus
interfered and pulled me away from reality. Action pulled me
back. As a by-product of that action, shyness disappeared for
the moment from my awareness. And shyness that isn't in your
awareness is never a problem.

I am not suggesting that you deny or ignore your anxieties. I
am saying that going on about your business of living, bringing
your attention back to the tasks at hand (the requirements of
the situation), will result in the pleasant side effect of less shyness. Someday, with much practice, it absolutely will not matter
to you whether you are feeling shy or not. You'll be able to
make the date, make the speech, do the shopping, propose,
demand, refuse, whatever, however you are feeling at the time.
That's the secret of overcoming shyness. It is really overcoming
the interference of shyness in daily life. That's what maturity is
all about—not feeling confident all the time but doing what

needs doing regardless of your feelings. Incidentally, the shy feelings will eventually fade—you just won't have time for the self-indulgence of noticing them. You'll be too busy living.

Depression

I have another identity. My other self even has a name: David Kent. We chose that name because my full name is David Kent Reynolds, so David Kent is a part of me. Several years ago Norman Farberow and I received a grant from the National Institute of Mental Health to create a depressed, suicidal person and send that researcher/patient into various psychiatric facilities in order to experience them from the inside. David Kent is the person we created. The staffs of these facilities gave permission to have a researcher/patient live in, but they didn't know who he would be or when he would enter their institution.

I had to learn how to make myself depressed—an unusual task, to be sure. Then I had to learn how to bring back David Reynolds when the research was completed. Perhaps you are wondering whether it is possible to develop such a "skill" at all. Well, descriptions of Kent's experiences are detailed in a couple of books, *Suicide: Inside and Out* and *Endangered Hope*. Let me say here that the psychiatrist who treated Kent on a mental hospital ward had previously attended a lecture by Dr. Reynolds, yet she did not recognize that these two people were housed in the same body. Furthermore, psychological tests showed Kent to be depressed, the hospital records agreed, and Kent, of course, felt just awful. All indications were that Kent was experiencing true depression.

I've worked with case files and patients in the VA system and at the Los Angeles Suicide Prevention Center for years, but the experience of researcher/therapist needed to be supplemented by the experience of researcher/patient before I could write with confidence about depression. Let me begin by describing how to make yourself depressed. Knowing how to become depressed is important for two reasons. In the first place, you can avoid doing what it is that gets you into this state when you want to avoid it. Furthermore, the methods for getting Kent out of his depression after the research was over involved doing more or less the opposite of what was done to create Kent.

Depression can be created by sitting slouched in a chair, shoulders hunched, head hanging down. Repeat these words over and over: "There's nothing anybody can do. No one can help me. It's hopeless. I'm helpless. I give up." Shake your head, sigh, cry. In general, act depressed and the genuine feeling will follow in time.

Feelings *follow* behavior. That principle is emphasized throughout the book. Influence feelings through purposeful behavior. It was what I *did* (sitting a certain way, breathing in a particular manner, repeating phrases of despair to myself) that produced the mood for Kent. Later on, merely going on the wards where Kent had been hospitalized and sitting in the dayroom chairs in which Kent had sat was sufficient to create strong gusts of depressive emotions. Putting ourselves in certain locations can restimulate feelings.

What did we do to bring back David Reynolds after the research was over? First, Kent had to become physically active— even though he didn't feel like it. Kent wanted nothing more than to hide out in some dark quiet corner lost in his self-pity and sorrow. Try sitting down for a whole day and see what it does to your mood (not to mention your intestinal tract). Brisk walks, tennis, and jogging helped. Increased stimulus of all sorts was necessary. Cheery music and bright colors made a difference. It also helped to interact with friends who knew my healthy identity and expected me to be active and alert. Fresh scenery and fresh clothes helped mark the change.

David Kent didn't *want* to do any of these things. On some level he knew they were necessary, though, so he tried them even if he wasn't in the mood for all that excitement and change. Then, once he was caught up in the activity, he began to change. What *he* began to desire and appreciate started merging with *my* needs and lifestyle until he became me again.

The point of this discussion is simple. When you feel depressed, the tendency is to depress yourself further by inactivity and recycling negative thoughts. Washing dishes, a walk, table tennis, almost any constructive activity will help, even though you don't feel up to it at first. The behavior itself lifts the mood.

Some depressions continue until there are chemical changes that need to be brought back into balance. In this case there are effective antidepressants which can be prescribed by your physician. The activity involved in getting to the doctor's office is good in itself. Minor depressions are best outgrown through character development and life management along the lines described in this book. Serious depressions involving severe loss of appetite, troubled sleep, suicidal impulses, lethargy, and lost sexual drive should be handled by competent professionals. The methods suggested in this book can be carried out simultaneously with therapy.

One principle was clearly confirmed by our research in psychiatric settings: the fluctuation of feelings over time. When people go into a depression it seems to them that they're facing something that will continue unchanged forever. They face everlasting sorrow, abandonment, hopelessness. Yet, in fact, in the deepest depression there are ripples and waves of somewhat lighter moods. Perhaps these cycles are based on biorhythms. At any rate the slight upturns can be ridden like waves to higher, more pleasant feelings if you move with constructive activity. Some mornings we wake up a bit more energetic than others. These mornings provide the initial foothold; but, remember, the ultimate goal is to do well no matter how we feel. Therein lies a long-term purpose worthy of a mature man or woman.

A final note from our research. Kent came across two types of people who tried to help him with his depression. One type tried to *pull* him out of his sorrows. "Cheer up!" they advised. Of course, if Kent could have cheered up, he would have. But he couldn't change his feelings by willing them to change any more than his would-be helpers could. We can't directly control our own feelings; certainly we can't directly control any one else's feelings. So these helpers didn't really help. They made Kent feel even more like a failure when he couldn't cheer up as they advised. He thought they didn't really understand what it's like to be depressed. He began to feel guilty about feeling sad. Sometimes Kent thought they wanted him to cheer up not for his sake but for theirs.

The second type of helper was much more effective. These people simply sat with Kent and allowed him his feelings. They were available and supportive when he was ready to be active; but they did not try to force him to fit their pace of life, even for his own good. They allowed him time to get to know his sadness well, even to treasure it. They built a social relationship by being there. They seemed to understand that Kent's emotions, however tormenting, would clear at their own tempo allowing opportunities for constructive action.

Fear and Stress

Anyone who says he isn't afraid of anything is both stupid and lying. Fear is a healthy emotion. It produces caution, and caution helps keep us alive. Fear, like pain, is unpleasant for anyone, but the discomfort is an alarm that calls our attention to some problem facing us. It is good to be afraid at times. Fear can help us survive, quite literally.

Let me introduce some people who were very surprised to learn that their fears were all right. Michelle was deathly afraid of having cancer. Her mother and aunt had both died in middle age of cancer and Michelle was approaching forty. She went regularly for checkups and sought specialists to find the malignancy that she knew must be growing somewhere within her. No one could find any signs of cancer. Her worries grew as she considered her hidden tumor. One specialist told Michelle she had a cancer phobia. She needed psychiatric help, he advised, not an oncologist. A medical technologist friend of hers jokingly called her a "crock" and hinted that Michelle's problem was all in her mind. But no matter what the young woman tried, she couldn't make her fear go away. Moreover, she now began to worry about going crazy.

Why couldn't she get rid of these unreasonable thoughts and feelings? Michelle felt guilty and worried about being afraid. Whole new layers of worry began to pile up. As Michelle told her story she looked disheveled, her hands trembled, her eyes were downcast and tearful. Her body looked rigid from the effort of holding herself together. She wondered what to do about the fear that had troubled her so. She seemed startled when I suggested that fear of cancer was not her problem at all. I'm afraid of cancer, too. Everyone ought to fear it. Being afraid of cancer prompts us to have checkups, watch the kinds of food we eat, work to get rid of carcinogenic substances in water and air. Fear of cancer has motivated medical scientists to conduct lifesaving research projects; it has moved families to take out health insurance. Cancer is a fearsome disease. Why *not* be afraid of it?

Michelle's problem was not her fear of cancer. It was the way she allowed this fear to intrude upon what she needed to do in her daily life. In the future she needn't waste energy trying vainly to overcome a natural fear. Instead she could direct her attention toward getting her hair brushed, showing up regularly for work, preparing her meals, and so forth—all the while accepting her phobia as it is. In time she might even come to be grateful for it.

How strange! All the while she had been focused on the desire that she *shouldn't* have cancer, that she *shouldn't* be afraid of it, that she *shouldn't* feel so worried about her unreasonable fear, that she *shouldn't* be who she was, she had pretty much removed herself from normal day-to-day living. The more she redirected herself toward the business and play of living in the now, the less she noticed her extreme fears. Michelle does volunteer work these days in the spare time she can set aside from a rich and busy life. Her volunteer work is with an agency investigating the health hazards of nuclear waste disposal. Michelle is still afraid of cancer. Good for her!

Carlos got a promotion. He's now in charge of his section at the phone company, and he's scared to death. He has worked incredibly hard for this position; but now that it's his, Carlos doubts that he can handle it. Of course he didn't tell anyone at home or at the office about his apprehensions.

What exactly is he afraid of? Well, he says, there are section leader meetings he must attend, and he doesn't feel comfortable with those people. Furthermore, he must make hiring decisions and reprimand errant employees and make sure his section meets the stepped-up quotas that forced his predecessor to retire early. Then there are increased work hours—his wife doesn't like that—and the fellows he used to work with seem cool and even critical of him now. The pressures are all converging on Carlos; he's afraid he can't handle them all.

Carlos's story is not unusual. You might be surprised to learn that not only demotion but promotion can precipitate a suicide attempt. Stress comes with success as well as with failure.

Carlos's first problem is the same one we've seen again and again in this book. He thought that he *shouldn't* feel the way he did. Then he tried to make the feeling go away. It has always intrigued me that many clients need an authority figure to give them permission to go ahead and feel what they're already feeling. Hey, Carlos, you're feeling stressed, doubtful about yourself in this job, worried about these new responsibilities! It's okay to feel that way! Changes often bring feelings like that. They're natural, they're even good, in a way, even though they're unpleasant. Stress makes us alert in new situations. It prompts us to behave cautiously and make efforts to diminish the stress. When we're scared, our body and mind are hyped up for some response—that is, we are primed to *do* something.

Pressures and stresses that continue over a long time can eat away at our minds and bodies. Ulcers, high blood pressure, irritability, sleep problems, decreased resistance to all kinds of illness, and so forth—these are the possible results. The cause of these terrible consequences lies neither in the environmental stressors nor in the feelings they produce. The cause lies in the long-term lack of success in acting to change the situation. When you don't do anything to change what is happening, when you just sit in the pressure cooker with the burner turned up high, when you don't build or learn or move or oppose or educate or otherwise respond to your circumstance, you are in for trouble unless kindly Fate steps in and turns the burner down for you.

Carlos didn't wait for a miracle. He talked to some section leaders about how they felt when they attended *their* first meetings and was gratified to learn they had felt as confused as he did. He studied business psychology and management arts. He made an effort to get to know everyone in his section and to let them know something about himself as a person as well as a supervisor. He gathered statistics to show management that their quotas might be possible but not with current personnel levels and not without new skills training.

To be sure, life didn't suddenly turn rosy for Carlos when he began accepting his feelings and getting on with business. But somewhere along the line, with the studying and listening to complaints and gathering data for statistical reports and rebuilding ties with his former coworkers, he just sort of forgot about being afraid that he wasn't big enough for the job. Once in a while the self-doubts pop up again. Carlos wonders if someone else might not be able to do what he is doing with less effort and better results. Perhaps so. Nevertheless, Carlos has decided to limp along until he can walk with assurance. It sure beats hiding out under a blanket of self-doubt and timidity.

Grief

Grieving not only follows the death of a loved one. People grieve for many kinds of loss. The loss of a home in a fire, the loss of youth, the loss of a long-term job, the loss of a limb, separation, divorce, failing eyesight, a missed opportunity—all these experiences may induce grief. Furthermore, the grief can even precede the loss. I see anticipatory grief in the families of patients with fatal illnesses and in the patients themselves, for they too are about to lose their loved ones (the survivors) and everything else they have marked with their living.

What we grieve for, when we grieve, how long we grieve, and the way we grieve varies from person to person, from situation to situation, from culture to culture. But knowing that we have learned our expression of grief from those around us gives very little comfort in the cauldron of sorrow, helplessness, anger, loss, abandonment, and exhaustion following personal disaster.

Those who try to ignore, suppress, or deny their feelings of grief often run into trouble later. In my research on psychological response to natural disasters (floods, tornadoes, earthquakes, and the like) it was not uncommon to find people who came to mental health professionals six months or a year after the disaster. They said they had gotten through the disaster very well—better than anyone else, it seemed. They were pillars of strength for their family and neighbors. They filled out the necessary papers, cleaned up the debris, and rebuilt. They may have felt a bit shocked or numb, or washed out, but they report that they never felt despondent, never cried, never asked for comfort from others. In a sense, they had put a lid on their feelings. So what brought them for mental health counseling later?

The strangest thing was happening, they said. Now that everything was over and it was back to business as usual, they found themselves with problems that made them wonder if they were losing their minds. They had insomnia or they broke down crying because a check didn't arrive in the mail on the day it was expected or they suddenly started lashing out at the family dinner table. It's not like me to be this way, they lamented. Am I going crazy?

These people were paying the price for putting a clamp on feelings, for trying to control uncontrollable emotions. They needed to get in touch with their emotions during the disaster; then the delayed outbursts of emotion would be unlikely to occur. In any case, delayed or timely, what bursts forth needs to be accepted while we go on with living.

On the other hand you may know of people who make the opposite mistake of "letting it all hang out" in an uncontrolled downpour of sorrow and despair. Six months or a year after some terrible loss they are still weeping at the office, still retelling the tragic story to those who have heard it many times already, still dependent on others to take care of meals and housework, still obsessed with the past.

How can we find a healthy middle ground between these two extremes of suppression and excess? First, it is important to recognize and accept feelings of loss and despair as much as any other feelings. There is no reason to try to control the emotions connected with grief. In fact, the effort only makes matters worse. When we lose something important, we ought to feel sorrow for the loss. The lost person or object *merits* our grief. To feel deeply is to be human.

Sorrow passes with time as does every other emotion—unless, of course, the feeling is restimulated by some act or event. After my father died, my mother felt the loss deeply but in time the sharpness of the hurt diminished . . . until the day came to clean out his closet and dresser, then Christmas, his birthday, their anniversary, a photograph turning up unexpectedly in the back of a desk drawer. All these circumstances brought back nostalgic and painful memories. In time, though, these too faded into the background.

Those who are wise soon return to handling everyday responsibilities without pretending that they are feeling better or worse than they actually are. They don't try to *hide* from their feelings in busyness and frantic activity. But they find that being active is more likely to pull their attention out of sorrow than lying in bed or collapsing in a chair. People who are frantically busy are suspect; people who so desperately need to be helpful that they force their service on others should also examine their purpose. Nevertheless, a full retreat from life helps no one.

Even after a great loss, we face moment-by-moment situations that need our thoughtful response. Focusing on the situation and acting intelligently, all the while accepting the naturalness of the grief, is the healthy way to live through rough times. Others have done it. We all have the power to do it. And when the worst has passed we have gained confidence that in those awful times we felt deeply without falling apart. How much easier, then, it will be to behave responsibly in the gentler times ahead.

In other words, we have the power of character growth through suffering. More than one culture emphasizes the possibilities of maturing through suffering. Grief doesn't automatically bring qualities of strength, depth of character, and empathy. It is the *response* to grief that enables us to grow. To survive a loss in every positive sense is to have made a crucial step toward growth as a human being . . . an important step toward preparing one's self for living fully now and for losing everything ultimately in death.

What needs to be done? It may be best to seek temporary comfort from friends. Many people hesitate to ask for help. But wouldn't you gladly offer yourself in service to your friends if they were suffering? Give them a chance to help if you need them. One of the inspiring results of otherwise dreadful disasters is the strengthened ties within families and communities as people pull together through rough times and learn to count on themselves and each other.

Chronic Pain and Chronic Illness

Carl overdosed on persimmons. Yes, persimmons. You see, Carl's kidneys weren't functioning properly. He had to come into a local hospital for dialysis once a week. He knew that persimmons had a lot of potassium, more than his kidneys could handle, but he went on a binge that brought him to the emergency ward in an ambulance.

Why did he do such a crazy thing? Carl himself wasn't sure. A middle-aged craftsman with a good family and fine medical care for his chronic kidney problem, he had a lot to live for. Perhaps he was tired of the weakness and tired of the pain from the shunts that hooked him to the machines for blood purification. Perhaps the strain of keeping on a diet, watching his exercise, and keeping the shunts immaculately clean had begun to wear on him. Perhaps he just craved persimmons that day. At any rate, Carl ate of the fruit and very nearly died.

Another lady I know, Laura, has chronic back pains that confine her to bed for weeks at a time. She has tried traction, bedrest, braces, pills, injections, even hypnosis. The pain comes and goes pretty much regardless of the treatments. Sometimes she feels so depressed she thinks of ending it all. Over forty now and living with her mother and father, she despairs of ever marrying. Who, she wonders, would want to take on the burden of an invalid wife?

With the conquest of most infections and parasitic diseases, more and more medical time and money is being spent on treatment of chronic illnesses for which "cure" in the old-fashioned sense is impossible. Management of the disease becomes our goal. As people survive into old age, long-term debilitating diseases eventually have their day. As we claw and scratch for longer life, our fingernails inevitably weaken and break off.

Chronic illness and pain, like neurosis, are forms of suffering. In order to make them bearable, you have to begin by accepting these conditions as they are. I don't mean to stop looking for a cure and I don't mean to stop treatment and I don't mean to give up finding realistic ways of living with the problem. By accepting the condition I mean that you must stop wasting energy wishing it would go away, pretending you're not handicapped by it, wondering what life would have been like without it, cursing God or Fate for letting it happen to you, or otherwise letting yourself be distracted from facing up to the situation that life has brought you.

You don't like it. Of course you hurt! Yes! Now what needs to be done? There's a fascinating book edited by Anselm Strauss, *Chronic Illness and the Quality of Life,* which deals with the practical adjustments people have had to make in order to handle the new situations created by their disorders. Their daily lives require rescheduling and new pacing of activities, rerouting of market trips in order to utilize wheelchair curbs or to avoid hills, arrangements for backup support in case of accident, education so that families can help intelligently, dietary control, skill in recognizing changes in their own bodies, rearranging furniture for accessibility to equipment and medications, adjusting bathroom and bed facilities at home, changes in exercise habits, contact with others who share the same difficulty, and much more.

Illness sets up a new set of constraints and possibilities for life. To be alert to the life rules which apply to the reality of the moment, to respond positively to the options available, to lose one's self in the *doing* of what needs doing—that is the way to a satisfying existence. People who moan endlessly about what is happening to them, lost in their misery and self-centered despair, focus almost exclusively on their own suffering and thus feel it more acutely. They actually hurt more, subjectively, than their counterpart who has precisely the same disease but lives constructively.

If there's anything that pain does very well, it is to bring us back to the here and now and force us to find meaning in the present. The crushed thumb asks: What is happening *now?* Why is my leg aching? What did I do to make my stomach upset like this? Life is easy to drift through when things are going well, but a quick shot of pain brings us up short. And longer periods of hurting force us to explore the meaning of life and the meaning of suffering.

Any religion or ideology worth its salt offers meaning in every moment of life—including moments of suffering. Christianity, for example, offers the believer the possibility of making every act an act of worship, every word a prayer. Singing in a choir, parking a car, visiting a dying patient, even urinating—all can be done in a uniquely Christian manner. All have potential for being acts of worship, offerings to God. Pain can be accepted as an act of submission to God's will; it can be used to develop empathy for Christ's suffering and for others' pain in this world. Illness and health both fit into the Christian view of God's scheme of things in this world.

Freudian thought is a belief system, too. It offers meaning in every moment of life because each thought, feeling, and act furnishes us with information about ourselves. Even a mistake at the typewriter keyboard or a slip of the tongue provides data for self-understanding. And self-understanding or insight is what Freudian psychoanalysis is all about.

What meaning does Morita's system of thought offer? I suggest to you that every situation, every moment, provides the opportunity for self-growth and development of your character. Reality keeps bringing us circumstances—sometimes I picture them as waves breaking on the shore—and we have the chance to keep merging with that reality, to fit ourselves to it, to dive into those waves. If we simply stand and let the waves crash over us, if we mistime our dive or plunge at the wrong angle or try to flee from the waves, we get battered around by their force. But a clean dive sets us up for facing the next series of waves. Afraid or not, we dive into the wave. Hurting or not we dive. Weak or not we dive. In time the biggest breaker holds no fear for us, because our perceptions are sharp and our diving skills are sufficient for even the tidal wave of death.

I happen to know that it is possible to die well. I've spent a lot of time conducting research on wards for terminally ill patients and talking with people in nursing care homes for the chronically ill. I've interviewed patients who were dying and staff members who had worked with dying persons for years. I know, therefore, that some patients pass away skillfully. That is a remarkable feat because almost no one has the chance to *practice* dying. Somehow, though, these people seem to develop the skill, the knack of dying well, during their lifetime of living.

These people have learned to accept the reality that faces them and carry on as best they can. Often these dying patients are the ones who are comforting their families and friends rather than the other way around. But, then, aren't they displaying precisely the acceptance and personal commitment to purposeful behavior that this book is all about? Isn't dying just another circumstance of living? The reality of the hospital bed, the nightstand, the tray, the visitors, the blood tests and drugs and bed pans and early morning awakenings—all require a constructive response. One dives into the hospital wave just as one dives into the school wave or the housework wave or the divorce wave. The circumstances are different, but the diving skills are the same.

It is the recognition that doing is one aspect of living which has led behavioral scientists to emphasize that the *quality* of a patient's life should not be sacrificed while keeping him alive longer. Medical science has become adept at prolonging life. To some degree the patient's environment—even his inner environment (pain, hunger, thirst, and the like)—can be influenced by the staff members and others who are there to care for him. But even an ideal environment (and for one reason or another the environment never is ideal) cannot satisfy the patient who is unprepared to die. What you are doing now, what you will do five minutes from now, and tomorrow, and next week, will prepare you for this final circumstance of living. My wish for you is that you train yourself persistently and well, and that you begin right away.

We all fear death and fight actively against it. That survival instinct is a natural and sensible attribute of our species. Hold your breath for a few minutes. Notice the discomfort and driving urge to get the air flowing again. Your body struggles against death every day whether you will it or not.

Morita believed that this basic abhorrence of death corresponds to a general fear of failure and loss of all kinds. He said, moreover, that the opposite side of this abhorrence is the positive drive to succeed, to experience broadly, to develop our potential. Without this fear of death, without our survival instinct, we would have no desire to live fully and well. Morita called this single dimension ranging from survival to self-actualization *sei no yokubo*—literally "craving for life." I'm not sure that our need to live well grows out of our survival instinct. Yet, certainly, both are basic to humanity.

What is the consequence of having this basic need for self-development? When our drive to succeed meets with our recognition of reality (including our own handicaps) we are likely to get upset, to feel depressed and inferior, to have neurotic moments. But if we get distracted by these upsetting feelings, if we focus strictly on ourselves, we achieve even less of what we set out to do. Then we get even more dissatisfied, more self-centered, more neurotic. As we have seen, the goal of Constructive Living is to accept the desire to live fully, accept all the reality that life brings us, and get on about the things we can *do* . . . including the things that will change reality for the better.

Lack of Energy

Are you tired all the time? No enthusiasm? Since the most obvious possibility is some sort of physical problem, a physician should be consulted in order to rule out disease. But suppose that possibility has been checked out by your doctor. No anemia, no infection, nothing apparently wrong with the body at all. You are getting enough sleep (perhaps even too much), your diet is adequate, but you just don't feel up to doing much of anything. There may be minor headaches, stomach problems, backaches, and the like. Your head and limbs feel heavy at times. Sometimes parts of your body tingle or go to sleep. You may be bothered by a ringing in your ears. You have little appetite. Your eyes tire easily. You're stiff. No matter how much rest you get you continue to feel exhausted.

One of the first things we work on when a client brings problems like these to our training sessions is exercise. No medical indications to the contrary, we start on long walks and work up to jogging or other active sports. But how can you exercise when you're feeling so tired? Tired or not, you walk. Surprisingly, the exercise seems to *generate* energy rather than to drain it. Sleep improves; appetite sharpens.

Next we work on cutting down rest periods during the day. The circumstances of daily life vary from person to person. Some people need more sleep than others. But a short break each morning and afternoon is sufficient rest during the day. Whenever possible, I take a thirty-minute nap in the afternoon and wake, without an alarm, refreshed and alert. Other people prefer different patterns of effort and rest. Most of the people I see use sleep and rest as escapes from their dreary daily routines or relief from anxiety-producing situations. They need to learn the Constructive Living lesson that refreshment can come from switching from one task to another. The movement from job to job during the day keeps us interested and involved in the activity rather than in ourselves.

Again, the perpetually exhausted person is self-focused. All the minor bodily complaints arise because this person's involvement is only with himself. With the attention turned inward, any minor disturbance in bodily functions is exaggerated. We all have ringing in our ears to some degree if we stop to notice it. There are minor aches and stiffness in everyone's body. The secret is to be too busy living to notice them.

We can start this involvement in Constructive Living with exercise. There is something about the actual movement of our bodies that pulls our attention to the activity at hand. When I'm upset, it is easier to get into digging up a garden than it is to lie down and read a book. When I'm sleepy, I can get involved in a game of table tennis easier than I can keep tuned into a television set. When I'm tense, it's more satisfying to take a walk than to sit writing in a chair. To be sure, humans (crafty creatures that we are) use this principle of activity to sidestep problems that need to be faced squarely and resolved. We are capable of running away—literally—from some of our life problems.

Nevertheless, for the person who lacks energy, physical exercise is good in itself. Ruminating over our poor psychophysical state simply spirals us toward depression and more preoccupation with the body. Hiking, jogging, softball, and other sports pull us into the world outside.

After an exercise program is under way, my next suggestion is to work hard. At the office, the assembly line, the school, or at home, put effort into doing even the most routine tasks as perfectly as possible. The way we form letters and numbers as we write, the preparation of an exquisite salad, the most efficient movements, purposeful conversations, well-planned breaks, thoughtful acts of service—every action should be carried out with awareness and full attention. Of course, we all forget our resolutions sometimes; we drift into old patterns of mindless habit. Working hard and well takes years of concentration.

The next step is to use our newly found energy for other people. It's amazing what wellsprings of vigor are available to people who truly give themselves to those around them. A rural schoolteacher I know celebrated her golden wedding anniversary and retired from teaching in the same year. Where did she get the vitality to keep up with her first graders even when she was well beyond the normal retirement age? What keeps workers going for days without sleep in times of disaster or crisis? The body may demand recuperation later, but during the involvement there is remarkable focus and apparently unlimited energy.

In sum, then, for the sort of nervous exhaustion described here I recommend what seem at first to be some very unnatural attitudes and behavior. Don't pamper yourself. Do get active. Do stay busy. Do find ways to help others rather than keeping an exclusive focus on yourself. Remember: If you have to be perfect before offering help to those nearby, you will never lend a hand. Don't wait to feel up to something before giving it a try. Your body is your servant, not your master. So, feeling masterful or not, zippy or unzipped, aching or numb, get going!

Troubled Romance and Marriage

Love is a feeling like any other feeling. We cannot control it by an act of will. Yet it need not be allowed to push us around. Sometimes love is convenient; sometimes it is an impediment to what we need to do in life.

It is all very dreamy and romantic to speak of a lifetime obsession with love; it is rather adolescent, as well. Love comes and goes. It fades in time unless restimulated. Whatever the fairy tales say about princes and princesses living happily every after, a romance alone is a shaky foundation indeed for a long-term relationship.

To write about this glorious feeling in such a cool way seems heartless. I am not heartless. I am realistic. Unless your behavior remains under the control of your good sense, romance will lead you into trouble and then slip away, leaving you with memories and regrets. On the other hand, intelligent behavior can shape infatuation into something deeper and more lasting. We grow a love as we grow a plant. And in the nurturing action we nurture ourselves. Let's see what I mean.

Mabel and Ralph have been living together for nearly ten years. They have a marriage of sorts. Recently, though, they have been fighting nearly every day. She threatens to leave, but both feel that the relationship is worth saving if their problems can be worked out. What are the complaints? The list seems endless. He is untidy and undependable; she is harsh and sexually demanding. Who is to prepare meals when both are working? Who pays which bills? She says he has a sloppy appearance and bulging waistline; he complains of her chronic exhaustion and perpetual bad humor. And so on and so on and so on.

Now I see nothing wrong with getting family members together to work on the problems they create for each other. But I prefer to work with the members of couples or families individually as well as together. Why? Because I don't want them to lose the chance to grow individually. The partner may die tomorrow or leave or be changed in some unpredictable way (by a virus or a speeding auto or sudden fame). The principles of Constructive Living can be used to handle that reality or any other. If the focus is on the couple or family group, what's to be done if the group regroups or a breakup occurs or a new member joins?

After the first session with Mabel and Ralph together I made appointments to see them separately. Right from the start I make it clear that I see no one at fault in the problems they face. No one is to blame. But I'll need their cooperation to solve the problems, each working as if he or she were the sole cause of the difficulties. Okay, Ralph, let's get to work.

Ralph, like most people who are having trouble at home, seems to want me as his ally in his struggle against Mabel. Mabel, of course, wants me on her side. Well, Ralph, I'll be your ally in a different sense. I'll help you become a person more worthy of Mabel. I'll help you appreciate and love her more. Here's what I want you to do.

We start with a surprise present and a secret act of service each week. Ralph is to get something for Mabel, wrap it himself, and present it to her. We agree on an approximate weekly cost. He doesn't have to feel like buying it or giving it to her. He doesn't have to feel that she deserved it. Buying, wrapping, and giving are enough. Ralph is also instructed to do something for Mabel without letting her know that he did it. The act of service must not benefit Ralph directly in any way. We agree on the amount of time he should invest in this service each week. Say fifteen to thirty minutes. It is most effective to perform this service when he is angry at Mabel, but any time is acceptable. Next, each evening Ralph is to make a list of what Mabel did for him during the day and also the troubles he caused her. He is not to list what he did for her or the problems she caused him.

Each week we review Ralph's gift, service, and lists. We work on the means by which Ralph can present more thoughtful gifts, better service, and fewer problems for Mabel. Of course, Ralph initially wants to unload about Mabel's inadequacies, their fights, his fears about a breakup, and so forth. After a few minutes of listening, I try to make it clear that I care so much about these upsetting events that we had better get to work on solving them. And back we come to the gift, the service, and the lists.

Can you see how these changes in behavior bring about changes in Ralph's attitude? Of course, over the weeks Mabel is receiving the same instructions during individual sessions and carrying them out to Ralph's benefit.

Essentially, then, these are my suggestions for keeping a marriage in good running condition. Each spouse gives up part of his or her life for the other. Acts of service deserve words of appreciation. In a healthy marriage the air is filled with communications of politeness and gratitude. What can I do for you now? What do you think about this? Do you know how important you are to me? Of course, there are times when we are tired, unconcerned, and wish to be alone. Even then words of politeness, expressions of concern, and acts of service need not be neglected. Behavior is behavior. Whatever we are feeling, our partners deserve the finest. Then the feelings come to align themselves with the thoughtful behavior.

Now suppose you see a breakup looming ahead and you want to buffer the emotional effects of the inevitable loss. What would you do to prepare yourself for divorce? The natural distancing that takes place before a breakup is a kind of preparation for separated living. Do what you can for yourself and for those who will remain close to you. Keep your purposes clear. Accept your feelings of loss and abandonment, your self-doubts, your anxiety about the future. However you feel, keep on doing what you need to do. You may choose to grow a new love some day.

Love grown wisely and patiently presents a perfect opportunity to give up the self in a positive way. It is well worth the weeding, the watering, the shielding, the pruning. It is well worth the work.

Notes on
Constructive Living

THIS CHAPTER PRESENTS a series of short essays about various aspects of Constructive Living. The first essay deals with a way of evaluating whether one has mastered the principles. The second essay concerns the realistic limits of the method and what can be accomplished within those limits. In the third essay I consider an ambiguity the English language inserts between doing and feeling. Next, we look at the limits of conditioning, or behavior modification techniques. We cannot afford to overlook the situational flexibility necessary in behavior in order to live effectively.

The next essay, too, considers inflexibility. In this case, the permanence of labels or abstractions in the face of ever-changing reality presents potential obstacles to realistic living. The abstraction death is considered next—not as a verbal concept, but as an experience. The following essay points out broader perspectives on ownership, ideas, and effort while focusing on the craft of writing.

Subsequent brief essays deal with the fit between psychotherapy and culture, the strategies of chess and of life, giving oneself away, and the reasonableness of grounding one's life in behavior. Taken together the essays demonstrate some of the breadth of concerns stimulated by attention to Constructive Living.

Mastering the Principles

We have already met the young lady who believed she had mastered the principles of Morita Therapy in five or six weeks but was unable to find her way out of the building without assistance. Even after five or six weeks she hadn't noticed the route up two flights of stairs and around two corners. She wasn't paying attention.

Similarly, a young therapist remarked that the theory of Morita Therapy was rather interesting but he wasn't sure of its practical utility in his case. Then he learned that the personal check he had given for payment of our group meeting had been unsigned. He had forgotten to sign it.

A bright young woman invited me to lunch during a workshop and asked a series of penetrating theoretical questions about the relationships among Morita Therapy, Zen, and Christianity. In the middle of our discussion I asked, "How's your salad?" At that moment she understood a great deal about Morita Therapy! There is nothing wrong with intellectual understanding. But it need not be pursued at the expense of missing the experience of tasting one's salad.

What Are the Limits?

The strategy outlined so far is very effective for facing up to unpleasant situations and doing what needs to be done. Put simply, the general idea is to accept your feelings as they are and focus on behaving intelligently in the situation at hand. Developing these skills takes time and lots of effort, of course, and usually involves guidance or instruction. And the method does have its limits.

The method is limited, for example, when it comes to situations in which we are *realistically* unable to do what must be done. I emphasize the term "realistically" because again and again clients tell me that they just can't bring themselves to do what they know they have to do. "I just can't go up to him and ask for a date." "I just can't put a letter in the mailbox without checking the stamp and address six or eight times." "I just can't explain my side of the story when I'm accused of some error at work." These people give all sorts of reasons why those particular activities are impossible for them. At that time we need to review the uses of the word "can't" in the English language.

I *can't* leap out of this office window and fly to the tree across the street. I *can't* make myself seven feet tall. I *can't* corner the market on gold. These three sentences refer to a practical and realistic inability to accomplish the tasks. Most of my clients, most of the time, use "can't" in quite a different way. "I can't get on an airplane." "I can't stand up for my rights." "I can't break up the relationship with him." Notice that "can't" in *these* sentences means not an inability but an unwillingness and an unreadiness. It means "I won't," "I didn't," "I don't want to." Now I won't permit my clients to use the word "can't" in this latter sense during our time together. They must be clear on what is possible but difficult as opposed to what is truly impossible. We work hard on the troublesome areas that are possible but difficult.

Occasionally the problem does not involve behavior that is directly controllable. What needs to be done, as defined by the client, is something that is realistically and practically impossible. Such problems include trembling, sleeplessness, stuttering, and sexual impotence. All are forms of behavior, but they are unusual in that they cannot be controlled directly by the will. In this sense they are more like feelings than like other behavior. They form one limit of the methods described in this book.

Even though these problems aren't directly controllable, we don't have to give up on them. There are plenty of ways to attack them. The most obvious step is to use the same tactic we use with emotions—that is, accept them and stop struggling against them ineffectively. Usually, the harder we try to make ourselves go to sleep, the longer it seems to take. Stutterers often find that their problem gets worse when they bear down and strain to overcome the blocked speech. Similarly, not only do trembling and impotence rarely yield to pressure but they often become even more intransigent because of it.

Relaxed acceptance is the first step toward outgrowing these problems. If you stutter, you stutter. That's reality. That's you as you are right now. There are plenty of other things about you that are as important as your speech disorder. Get some perspective.

The next step is to do what you can. If your problem is impotence, pleasing your sexual partner is a worthy goal in bed. The sexually impotent man has all sorts of means at hand to offer affection and satisfaction to his partner. Sometimes, in the unselfishness of these offerings one's own capacities revive. This is not the place to go into a theoretical analysis of the causes of frigidity and impotence, but it is not uncommon to find them accompanied by an excessive concern for getting one's own share and a lack of interest in pleasing one's partner.

In cases of insomnia, going to bed (1) on a regular schedule, (2) in a place set aside for sleeping, and (3) having a presleep routine may be helpful. Your body will see to it that adequate sleep is attained provided there is no chemical imbalance produced by medication or by a severe depression or other serious psychiatric disorder. Most insomnia is merely a subjective problem caused by lying awake for seemingly endless hours without recognizing the catnaps that took place during the night and the bracketing days. When objectively measured, the actual hours of sleep are adequate for most insomniacs even though they say they don't remember getting any sleep at all.

Over fifty years ago Morita proved to one patient that he was, in fact, getting sleep during the night in spite of his protests that he wasn't slumbering at all. Morita had another patient call out to the insomniac at regular intervals during the night. Most of the time the calling produced no response. The sleepless patient was sound asleep.

Some people handle abnormally early morning awakenings

by getting up and writing letters, reading, and snacking, and then going back to bed later in the morning or after lunch. Others begin their sleeptime in the early morning hours because they find themselves lying awake for hours if they go to bed at ten or eleven at night. Study your life rhythms and try to adjust your sleep patterns to them. When such adjustments aren't feasible, you may be surprised to discover how smoothly you can adapt to another routine given time. I write more of routines than of variety (though both are important) because most of the people I see are pulled naturally toward variety, change, scatteredness. They need the stability of routine to overcome the tendency to be pushed around by feelings.

Trembling, writer's cramp, stuttering, and the like can influence people to avoid social contact. The housewife who worries about spilling her guest's coffee, the businessman who tries to sign contracts and checks in private so that no one will see his jerky movements, the stutterer who considers his speech an embarrassment to others as well as himself—all find their lives narrowed even beyond the immediate limits of their behavior problem. They closet themselves like lepers. Accepting themselves as they are and living as fully as possible is the initial step toward reducing their handicaps by outgrowing them.

Apart from the realistic limitation just mentioned, there are two formidable barriers to improvement using the techniques in this book. The first is lack of understanding. I cannot teach these principles to a small child, to a severely retarded person, or to an emotionally disturbed person who is so out of contact that my words are not sinking in. In this last situation, medication for psychosis or depression may be necessary to stabilize the clients' thought processes so that they can begin to learn what is being taught. But medication doesn't solve the practical problems of living discussed in this book; the hard work of overcoming these problems through accepting your feelings and managing your behavior remains for everyone.

The other barrier is not *wanting* to change. You might be surprised at how many people are hurting but don't want to
change their lives. Delinquents, alcoholics, drug abusers, and
violent people often talk about their unbearable suffering without making an effort to reduce it by changing their lifestyle.
More often than not they argue that their problem lies not
within themselves but in a harsh and unenlightened society,
uncaring and punitive parents, misguided friends, or bad luck.
These people aren't ready for Morita's methods. First they need
some sort of experience like that offered by religion, or love,
or Japan's Naikan therapy (see Reynolds 1983). They need to
rethink who they are and what their goals are in life. They need
to stop hiding from death. Confrontation with one's past (and
others' positive contributions to it) and one's future (and how
we can begin to repay our benefactors) is an important task for
everyone. There are effective means of accomplishing that task,
but that topic, too, goes beyond the focus of this book: the here
and now.

Thanksgiving Not Thanksfeeling

Occasionally one hears the client who has started a journal about
his dealings with others: what he has given, what he has received, the trouble he has caused. "I realize now," he will say,
"that I should feel more gratitude toward my parents (wife,
husband, girlfriend, boyfriend)." At this point I ask: "What do
you feel, though, when they are doing something for you?"

There is a difference between recognizing that others deserve
my gratitude and actually feeling that gratitude. The way to
reduce the discrepancy is, again, through behavior. Thanking
others, serving them, showing consideration for their conven-
ience more than my own, writing thank you notes, buying
token gifts, smiling your appreciation, offering the courtesies of

speech—these acts do not merely reflect gratitude but *generate* it when it is weak. One must be aware and poised to use these actions to create the desired feelings, and one must push against the inertia resisting constructive behavior. But the thanksgiving emotions will grow with thanksgiving behavior.

A social psychologist named Festinger proposed a theory of cognitive dissonance. Essentially he argued that if you act a certain way your attitudes will change to conform to the act. When a politically conservative student is assigned the task of arguing before his class a strong stand, say, against nuclear weapons, later his own attitudes will be found to have shifted toward the position he argued in front of the class. Furthermore, the *less* outside pressure or reward for doing it the *more* his attitude changes.

We are talking about the use of a similar dissonance to influence our *feelings*. "Behavior wags the tail of feelings" we say in Morita Therapy. We do, then we feel. The English language needs a neater way of distinguishing between, say, loving acts and loving feelings. When we say "she did loving things" or "she acted lovingly," the implication is that she felt loving feelings and then acted on them. I recommend phrases like "to *do* love," "to *do* patience," "to *do* courage," "to *do* assertiveness." They sound a little strange at first, but they mean that the *act* was loving (patient, courageous, assertive) whether the actor felt that way or not. Can you see the difference? To *be* courageous or to *feel* courage is not the same as to do courage. But often the doing will result in the feeling and being.

Conditioning Programs

Clients in conditioning programs are either rewarded or punished for certain kinds of behavior. An aversive conditioning program for weight loss, for example, might involve a painful electrical stimulus whenever the client smells or sees or touches high-calorie foods such as french fries. Eventually the client associates pain with french fries and avoids them.

The problem with conditioning programs from the Constructive Living point of view is that they don't allow the client to respond flexibly to changing situations. Suppose the overweight client develops a chronic disease that requires him to maintain his weight or even regain some weight. His *conditioning* continues to make him associate high-calorie foods with pain. He is in conflict with himself. On the one hand he knows he must eat these foods to keep alive. On the other hand there is discomfort when he even thinks about eating rich food.

In other words, conditioning works very well—maybe *too* well. The client is attracted to something or avoids something automatically in a mechanistic way. In fact, conditioning is based on a robotic model of humanity. Those who condition their clients and those who choose to be conditioned are not necessarily wrong for using conditioning to change behavior. But they are using a rigid and limited method of changing a specific kind of behavior. Wouldn't it be much better to change the behavior through self-discipline so the client can respond flexibly to a variety of situations? Eating more when it's appropriate, less when it's appropriate. Drinking a little here, not drinking at all there. Now careful, now assertive; now exercising, now resting. The variety and flexibility in response to life comes not with conditioning but with outgrowing one's problems.

Mislabeling

One young man, Arnold, came to the ToDo Institute with the fear that he was becoming a homosexual and the desire to work on his relationships with men. He was astonished to hear that there are no homosexuals and that he doesn't have relationships with men. What could I possibly mean by that?

Just as there are no neurotics, only neurotic moments, so there are only homosexual moments. The homosexual label implies a kind of permanence: an orientation that permeates every act of living. But such consistency isn't possible within that flow of awareness which spotlights us as now driver, now supermarket patron, now tennis spectator, now lover. Remember (better yet, check your experience again), it is the changingness that characterizes us.

Similarly, Arnold doesn't have relationships with men. "Relationships with men" is an abstraction, a shorthand way of talking about a lot of reality moments. In fact, Arnold shook hands with Ed at 2:15, waved goodbye to Bill at 4:30, and stared at a young man walking across the parking lot at 5:42. Furthermore, Arnold can't even "work on" those "relationships" because they have already come and gone. All Arnold has to "work on" is right here, right now. That's all any of us has.

I was well along in my anthropological training before someone pointed out to me that we aren't molded by society at all. Society doesn't force us to do anything. Society, like neurosis, is just an abstraction. It's a useful concept for sociologists and for folks who want to excuse their behavior. In fact, what reality brings us is Aunt Mary with her notions about good and bad, our parents who directed us toward the sort of life they considered best, the teachers and peers and coworkers who taught us (with or without awareness) what it is to be a proper member of society. It was these *individuals,* not some abstraction called society, that transmitted our socialization. The set of individuals who influenced you is different from my set, though we may have read the same seminal books and so forth. The point is this: We're influenced by real circumstances and real people, not by the abstraction "society."

There is, however, a strange way by which abstractions like "neurotic," "homosexual," "bad-tempered," "problem child," "hypochondriac," "nice girl," "lazy bum," "religious," and so forth can affect us. When we apply the labels to ourselves, believing them, we become more like the cardboard images they represent. The labels limit our recognition of flexibility— our ability to respond flexibly to what reality is bringing in this moment and the next.

So I wouldn't encourage Arnold to see himself as either heterosexual or homosexual (or bisexual, for that matter). He's much more than any of those. Whether he is shopping or sight-seeing or sleeping with someone I want him to do it well, with full attention. The issue is much greater than his sexual orientation: It is his life orientation. Just putting his sexual concern within that larger perspective resulted in some relief for Arnold.

The principles of Constructive Living apply in this young man's case as they do for anyone. The more he engages in homosexual behavior, the more he struggles with feelings, the stronger they'll hold onto his awareness. Accepting his shifting interests, thoughts, even his inner turmoil, he must go on about living.

One final point from our work with Arnold should be noted. He told me that as he hugged a man named Anselm during an encounter group he felt as if he were a young boy again hugging his father. A lot of emotion—attraction, awe, filial affection— emerged. Arnold seemed to find this event symbolic of some unresolved attachment to his father (or conflict with him). Perhaps this unresolved paternal relationship was contributing to his latent homosexuality, he mused.

I pointed out that Anselm is not Arnold's father and that Arnold is not a young boy. To say it required no great insight, but it came as a mild revelation to Arnold. The implication that I can only be what I am right now, that the baggage of the past can be discarded at will, seemed to surprise him. If he needed to straighten out something with his father, I advised, do so direct-ly. If the father is dead or impossibly distant, then what is there to do but accept the unfinished business of the past and get on with moment-by-moment Constructive Living now?

On Living Until We Die

People write and talk about "death." Death is a word, an abstraction, a concept. What is death like, we wonder? Is there a world beyond death? "Life and death itself is the life of the Buddha," wrote the Zen master Dogen Zenji. In *The Denial of Death* Ernest Becker reinterpreted psychoanalytic theory in terms of human powerlessness to prevent death. Richard Kalish and I wrote a book, *Death and Ethnicity,* about the different responses to death among ethnic groups in Los Angeles. Words, words, words.

We have images associated with death—images of hospital beds, corpses, funeral ceremonies, gravesites, mourning clothes, and the like. But our dying will not be an abstraction. It will be reality, experienced reality, for each of us someday. Not a word, not a general concept, but an experience. And that experience, like any experience, will take place in some context. My dying might be me-in-a-flaming-car-look-out-it's-going-to-explode or me-fading-away-slowly-I-can't-feel-anything-in-my-fingers-now or me-sharp-pain-in-chest-can't-breathe or whatever.

Constructive Living, in addition to training us for daily living, is part of our training for the moments of dying. We are living, after all, even while dying. We have considered the need to pay attention to life rather than merely passing through it: the necessity of living instead of just putting in time. Dying, too, provides the circumstance for attentive exploration of experience, at least for those last moments of consciousness. What needs to be done to prepare ourselves to merge with the situation presented by dying?

Living is rather like driving along a freeway. There are lane shifts, periods of braking, accelerating, turn indicators, defensive drivers—attention, all attention. Constructive Living is about paying attention to the flow of traffic, about fitting one's driving to the reality that presents itself—not passively but realistically, sensibly. It is merging with the flow or deciding to shift into an open lane slot, but always purposefully, always with awareness. Dying, too. Heading for the proper off ramp, downshifting, maneuvering so that you exit smoothly without disrupting the flow of traffic. Constructive Living is developing skill at driving even onto the off ramp of life.

Dying is neither good nor bad. It is just part of life driving: purposeful, destination-bound driving. All the while noticing the scenery. Professor Morita, dying in Japan, asked his students to watch the medical procedures performed on him. The students were struck with his effort to use even his last breaths to teach about being a human physician. But to Morita the teaching was natural, proper, what needed to be done, the only thing to do in that moment.

About Writing

One of my clients in counseling was a professional writer: young, idealistic, devoted to his craft, but beset by an agonizing problem. He had come up with an excellent idea for a novel. All through the night he sat at his typewriter roughing out a draft of his idea. For the next few days he talked about the story with his friends to see whether they thought it was as terrific as he did. After hearing the story, one friend suggested shifting the order—putting the middle of the tale in front in order to grab the reader's attention and create suspense early. The suggestion was brilliant! The more my client thought about it, the more he saw that the order in which he presented the story was crucial to its success. Yet at the same time he began to feel that the story was no longer his. After all, it was his friend's suggestion that really made the novel. He put off writing further drafts until he could overcome this moral dilemma. Was it still his story?

His friend made no claim on the work. He had only tried to be helpful. But my client struggled with his conscience. We talked for a while about what makes anything a possession. I pointed out that I have no idea where my thoughts come from. They appear out of nowhere and flash on the screen of my mind only to disappear and be replaced by other thoughts. Sometimes I can identify something that has been written or spoken before and credit is due those creators. But even then the order in which their works bubbled to the surface of my awareness, the context surrounding them, and the associated reflections are mysterious gifts from nothingness.

What makes a piece of writing "mine" is the effort of putting down word after word on paper. The investment of time and work in the writing makes the royalties and bylines legitimately mine—again, of course, with proper crediting of others' quotes and ideas.

I believe that the novel remains the creation of my young client. The more time he invests in refining it, the more it becomes his in the sense that he owns the tangible product of his behavior. The ideas, though, aren't his in the same sense. They come from people, books, films, from nowhere and from all around.

Certainly the young writer owes his friend something for his suggestion. He appreciates the suggestion and it is natural to express that appreciation: perhaps taking the friend to dinner, a thank you note, or a gift. Whatever expression of gratitude he chooses he must quickly get on with the writing. To get distracted by this issue is to succumb to a greater moral failure. He owes the world his novel. Given to him from nothingness (God, karma, whatever) he must not allow it to wither through his inactivity.

Times Have Changed

Freudian psychoanalysis grew out of the successful treatment of a kind of neurosis called hysteria. Hysteria doesn't mean "hysterical" in the sense of screaming and crying out of control. Hysteria is a particular kind of inability to make the body work as it should. Hysterical patients may be unable to see even though there seems to be nothing wrong with their eyes. Their arms and legs may feel paralyzed even though there is no apparent damage to their nervous systems.

What happened to the hysterical patients in Freud's day (and to the few hysterical patients we now see seventy or so years later)? It seems that some feelings and memories were so upsetting that the patients "forgot" or denied or otherwise avoided them. Somehow these hidden ideas and emotions found a way of expressing themselves by sabotaging the operation of the patient's body. I don't know how repressed anger or fear can make a person unable to walk or lift his hand in a threatening way. And no one else knows the neurophysiological mechanisms of such a condition, but there it is. Furthermore, Freud discovered that bringing these hidden thoughts and feelings back into awareness, into the conscious mind, usually made the symptoms disappear as if by magic.

In World War II some of our soldiers encountered such horror and danger in battle that their minds stopped registering reality and they ended up with hysterical paralyses, blindness, deafness to commands, and other forms of battle fatigue. Psychotherapists used hypnosis, drugs, and psychoanalytic techniques to bring back these repressed memories and feelings so the men could regain control of their bodies. The methods all worked rather well.

The difficulties, however, started when Freud began extending his effective techniques to neuroses that were not hysterias.

He and his followers tried them on people with phobias and obsessions, on broader psychosomatic problems like insomnia, ulcers, and nervous exhaustion. Psychoanalysts went on to try to "cure" criminals, psychotics who were out of touch with reality, and ordinary people who felt life was meaningless. Some even labeled whole societies sick and in need of psychoanalysis.

Freud's theory and method were pushed beyond their capacity to help. The insight, the recollections, the awareness that instantly cured many hysterics, too often failed to miraculously release the compulsion of a person who washed his hands every few minutes, the shyness of an adolescent, or the alcoholism of a long-term drinker. More and more patients walked around with some knowledge of the possible causes of their anxieties and a lot of knowledge about Freud's theories . . . but no relief, no control over their lives. They had insight. But they neither felt better nor acted more constructively.

And why should they? We don't cure pneumonia with a splint. Why should an effective treatment for hysteria necessarily work well for *all* psychological troubles? Of course it need not, and, in fact, it doesn't. Freud saw a lot of hysteria. We see less of it these days. One reason for the difference is the modern flood of self-knowledge and insight. Watch any television show lineup for a given night. You can see psychotherapists and family counselors being interviewed; you can view pop psychology on situation comedies, quiz shows revealing psych tidbits, even singers crooning lyrics connecting the psyche and the body. In other words, we know more in a superficial way about "getting our feelings out," not "bottling ourselves up," and "letting it all hang out." Times have changed since Freud's day. Hysteria is out of fashion.

We know the dangers of holding our feelings in or ignoring and suppressing them. But "going with the flow" of feelings and doing whatever feels right doesn't usually pay off either. Expressing our feelings can get us in a lot of trouble. Take the case of a student of mine. He liked to sleep in late but was always annoyed by his wife as she puttered noisily about the kitchen. He felt justified exploding at her because he had learned that it's wrong to keep anger inside. And she felt righteous indignation, too; after all she was preparing his meal. So she would yell back at him, he would leap from his bed, and they would find innovative ways of keeping the argument going for most of the morning. The aftermath continued for days. But they had expressed their pent-up emotions. Wasn't that the right thing to do? Then why did they feel so wretched for so long afterward?

The husband could have found a gentler way of communicating his dissatisfaction. A reasonable discussion might have eliminated the noise in the future. But would it have dealt with his annoyance that morning? I think so. First the husband must accept his annoyance as part of his reality. Then he must decide what needs doing about the reality of noise coming from the kitchen. Exploding at his wife might simply lead to resentful pot banging tomorrow. Telling her about the problem, asking for her cooperation, seems a more sensible way of getting done what needs doing. There is nothing inherently healthy about exploding and dumping one's frustration all over the bystanders. Angry or not we remain responsible for what we do.

Morita built his theories of neurosis and cure not on hysteria, as Freud did, but on obsession. Morita pointed out that any sort of neurotic problem attracts and holds the patient's attention. Whether the patient suffers from an extreme phobia of flying, anxiety about a possible heart attack, inability to study, constant fatigue, or the urge to return home again and again to be sure the gas is turned off, all these symptoms reflect an obsession with some problem, an intense turning inward, a *self*-centeredness.

That obsessing quality is inherent in neurosis today just as it was in Morita's time. It hasn't changed over the past seventy years because it is *essential* to all neuroses. Freud's notion of repressed feelings causing neuroses appears to apply to only a limited set of problems.

As Morita noted long ago, the opposite side of a crippling obsession with the self is a healthy turning outward to the environment, a losing of a self in constructive activity, an appropriate merging of the self with the situation at hand. It's almost a matter of definition. Where is your focus most of the time? Is it turned inward or is it turned toward the flow of reality that washes over you?

I believe we have entered an era in which we can no longer afford therapies that push for expression of feelings at the cost of responsibility. We cannot afford therapies that don't help clients outgrow their problems. Psychotherapies fit the times. In eras of affluence we find therapies that emphasize expressiveness and consumption—the conspicuous display of years of expensive psychoanalysis, for example. As resources decline we face again the limits of reality with no escape into carefree spending. Our natural resources and our basic environmental quality are declining as a result of years of self-centered unconcern and a self-expressive value system that ignored responsibility and service and patience.

Few people desire a government that tells each person what to do. Few feel comfortable with the thought of a dictator or a system of rigidly regulated living. Yet such conditions are the backlash we can expect to result from a "go with the feelings" society. Constructive Living puts responsibility for behavior right in the hands of the individual. We are responsible for what we do. At the same time, Constructive Living allows the freedom to feel and to recognize and even treasure the whole spectrum of feelings—the freedom to feel along with the responsibility to act properly. When enough people live that way the tight external constraints of big government become unnecessary. Maturity replaces the childish desire for totally pain-free living. We get done what we need to do.

Chess Problems and Life

I enjoy working chess problems, end games, mates in two, and the like. Underlying a chess strategist's enjoyment is, I think, a desire for truth. If the problem is well constructed, there is essentially only one correct solution, only one line of truth. It makes no difference whether the moves are made with anger or poise, whether the chess player is experienced or a novice, male or female, confident or timid—there are only the moves which lead to a solution and those which don't.

Many moves are possible, legal, even sensible. Yet only one line leads to checkmate. What needs to be done in order to win with precision is simply to make the proper moves. It is as easy and as difficult as that. Only the moves count. My present attitude, my childhood past, whether I've eaten or not, whether I'm loved or not, in the mood or out—it all comes down to making the proper moves.

That is life, too. The outcomes are not so clear in life, though. Life is played more as a whole chess game than as a circumscribed problem. Fate or Reality or God keeps making moves. We must keep responding while keeping our purposes in mind.

The Sensible Second Mile

In one of our Morita Therapy groups I offered some strange and unpalatable advice to several members. A young teenager complained about his stepfather's disinterest and strictness. I suggested he shine his stepfather's shoes twice a week. A middle-aged woman wondered how to get her wealthy brother to return thousands of dollars he had owed her for years. I advised her to send him still another fifty dollars along with a letter of apology for pressuring him to return the money all these years.

How peculiar! Such advice hardly makes sense. We live in an era of assertiveness and demanding one's rights. Yet the principle of the second mile holds today as it did in New Testament times. In those days Roman soldiers had the right to demand of subjugated Jewish citizens that they carry the soldier's pack for one mile. Traveling through the land was accomplished by finding a series of Jews to shoulder the Roman soldier's load single mile after mile. Jesus advised his followers not only to carry the burden the required mile but to voluntarily carry it a second mile! What in the world for?

Servitude and subjugation were the farthest things from my mind when offering advice along these lines. Service and voluntary self-sacrifice are quite different matters from servitude and subjugated passivity. One who walks a second mile *may* change the person whose load he carries. That result would be fine. But he is certain to change himself. That result is dependable. Control returns to his own hands. He frees himself once more.

Do you see why *choosing* to be a slave makes one free? Why *choosing* to throw good money after bad makes one rich?

The Culture Factor

Some people argue that because Morita was Japanese his methods must be useful only for Japanese people who are troubled in their lives. It can't possibly be effective in the cultural traditions of the West, they say. Such an attitude allows the critic to sidestep the fundamental issues posed by Morita's ideas about living. What is neurosis? What is cure? What are reasonable and attainable goals for therapist and client?

Other Eastern practices such as yoga, Zen, and transcendental meditation have found acceptance in the West despite cultural differences. Why not Constructive Living? The value of Constructive Living for Westerners is being tested by experience, not merely argued about with words. Thus far, our experience working with Western clients has produced encouraging results. It is true that practically any therapy shows initial success when first introduced. But Constructive Living has been in existence in Japan for over sixty years now, and it's still going strong. In the United States the broad application of Morita's insights is just now under way. Those of us who practice it see great potential for this method in the West.

Nevertheless, there are certain characteristics of Americans which make acceptance of these principles more difficult. Of course, not all Americans share these qualities, and, furthermore, some Japanese are much like Americans along these dimensions. Anyone, from whatever culture, who possesses these attributes in strong measure is likely to resist Morita's notions.

In the United States we are pressured to perform whether we are skillful or not. Mastery of a subject is valued, of course, and we may be able to improve our skills as we perform. But the emphasis is on turning out something right away. That's one reason why many writers and reviewer/critics are writing most of the time on subjects they know little about.

We are impatient. We want solutions now. Courses of action that take months or years to bring about change just aren't acceptable. We want instant judo, weekend enlightenment, ten-day tours of the Orient, accelerated degree programs, fast foods, fifty-minute television specials, brief news reports, condensed books, and so on. Such an attitude has produced breathtaking progress in some directions and rapid destruction in others. The quick divorce, the speeding driver, compulsory promotion of the slow learner, planned obsolescence, overmedication—all are examples of potential danger resulting from our obsession with the quick result.

Moreover, we lack courage. Fritz Perls wrote that Americans are afraid of pain. A good deal of energy goes into tranquilizing us chemically or helping us temporarily escape from confronting our pain through entertainment, sex, shopping, sports, and pop salvation.

And there is laziness. I wish I could think of a softer word for what prevents me from doing what I need to do sometimes, but the only word that seems to hit the mark is laziness. You see it in our bureaucracies, in the factories, in the schools. The goal of maximum pay for little or no work. The desire to advance without effort, to be the instant success, the overnight star.

Let us be honest here. Constructive Living offers a lifestyle of worth and dignity. But this mastery of life grows slowly, painfully, and only with effort. It requires attention, patience, self-discipline, honesty. It asks you to face your feelings, pleasant or unpleasant, to check out your purposes, large and small, to guide your own behavior, whatever the pain, in constructive directions. It advises you that when you fail, you must try again and again. It is in that very exertion, in that strain toward impeccability, that the suffering self is lost and a triumphant lifestyle is gained.

Behavior: The Bounded Ring of Order

On the inside there are uncontrollable feelings and sometimes controllable thoughts. On the outside is the external world: neither controllable nor just in any obvious way. The only area of control, then, is the area of behavior—disciplined behavior. It can be dependable even though feelings fluctuate and the external world sends reality careening to our senses.

Doing well—paying strict attention to what reality brings for us to do—provides the only stability. To be sure, feelings vary in ways that are sometimes regular and predictable. Similarly, reality generally follows natural laws as we discern them. Nevertheless, for me, now, knowing that there is a pattern does not ensure my control over either internal or external events. I may know something of the source of my obsession and still be obsessed. I may know about the physical laws governing pressures and temperatures inside a tire and still have a blowout on the freeway.

The regularity I see in other people is based strictly on their behavior. I need project no such concept as character or personality to explain their actions. One who does committing things is truly committed while acting. One who does courageous things is truly courageous while doing them, regardless of what he or she feels at the time. Consistency and truth, then, lie in behavior. It is "real" in a unique way. It displays itself in a way that links the internal and external. It ties flux to flux with the knot of choice.

Furthermore, it is reassuring that, like feelings, the results of my behavior lie outside the sphere of responsibility. Some of my friends have played the academic game diligently and well. They have taught and researched and published with some success. Yet because of economic and political pressures they find themselves without academic appointments after years of hard work. Some of them have become bitter about their professional experience. One complained to me: "I did everything I should have done for tenure, but it was denied me. It isn't fair." He is right; it isn't fair to see one's sincere efforts go unrewarded. But reality sometimes presents us with such injustice.

The emphasis in Constructive Living is on the doing itself. The rewards for teaching and research and writing are in the quality of the activities themselves, not in the end results. We hold purposes and goals for direction of behavior, but it is the *achieving,* not the achievement, that is valuable and controllable. Remember: Whether success or failure comes, reality *always* brings something to be done next. Reality always presents the circumstance wherein we can sharpen our self-application to action.

Exercises
and Applications

THE METHODS of Constructive Living come originally from the cold steel knife of Zen and the warm blanket of Shinshu Buddhism. But they have been employed for decades in Japanese psychiatric clinics and other mental health settings under the names Morita Therapy (Zen based) and Naikan (Shinshu based). In the United States these principles have been applied in secular Buddhist and Christian settings with little modification and much success. They are successful because they are practical. One need not profess a belief in some ideology; only an experiential try is necessary. If the methods don't work, they may be put aside like useless tools. But when they are found to be useful they set us on paths of growth that have no end in this life.

They are not psychotherapies in the sense of being useful only to bring someone "up to normalcy." They are of value to people at widely different levels of personal development, even to those whose lives are already on a sound footing.

So far you have read page after page expressing certain ideas about living, about success, about feelings and behavior. Probably at least some of the ideas made sense to you if you've come thus far in our thinking together. But words and ideas, important though they may be in outlining experience, are not in themselves sufficient. This part of the book suggests a number of exercises you can use to field-test the ideas I've been writing about. Without the validation of experience you are left with only a series of words and a tidy conceptual scheme. Since the final judgment of a lifeway requires some sort of validation, then, let's tack down these notions to reality.

Exercise I

I'd like you to start by observing the percolating productivity of your mind. Sit in a comfortable, quiet place by yourself. Place in front of you some object on which to focus your attention. It can be a vase, a painting, a fan, an old shoe, a piece of sculpture, a doll, a doughnut, anything. Then tell your mind to think only about that object for five minutes. Set an alarm or have someone call you when the time is up so that you don't have to keep checking a clock yourself.

Try to think only about the object you have selected. Soon you will notice some stray thought creeping into your awareness. Perhaps your attention has drifted to a pain in your body or a sound outside or a memory of an event that day or something the object of your attention reminds you of. When you realize that your thoughts have drifted, note what has welled up and then return your attention to the object. Soon your spotlight of consciousness will be elsewhere again. Again note the content of the drift and bring the spotlight back to the object. Again, as if it had a mind of its own, your unruly awareness will shift away. Patiently bring it back again and again until the time period is over.

Where do thoughts come from? I don't know. They bubble up from somewhere even as I try to direct them. Like feelings . . . like feelings. . . . This exercise is the basis for several of the subsequent guided experiences.

Exercise II

The second exercise hardly seems worthy of being called an exercise at all. I would like you to try eating, exercising, and sleeping regularly for a week. By regularly, I mean setting up a daily schedule that you follow for the whole week. Prepare balanced meals for yourself. Don't eat out. Don't let someone else cook for you. Don't make do with merely something cold from the refrigerator or something instant. If you are going to be away from home during the noon hour prepare a sack lunch that morning—thoughtfully. Put time and attention into food preparation. Then eat slowly without television or radio to distract you. And clean up the dishes if there are any immediately after eating.

See if your mind creates excuses for not sticking to your regimen. Notice the drifting currents of motivation just as you noticed your drifting thoughts in the first exercise. Feel like it or not, keep on preparing and eating on schedule.

Similarly, set aside at least thirty minutes for exercise each day. A thirty-minute stroll may be your limit. Add a few push-ups if you're capable. Then add skating, or weightlifting with chairs from the dining room set, or jogging, tennis, dancing, whatever gets your body moving and your blood flowing. Don't overexert yourself, don't ignore medical advice, but move about as best you can at a predetermined time and place.

Finally, set a reasonable schedule for sleep. Go to bed only when it's time to sleep. Don't read in bed. Get up as soon as the alarm goes off whether you feel like it or not. Even if you seem to lie awake all night, don't nap the next day.

What's the point of all this scheduled living for a week? There are several purposes. Eating, exercise, and sleeping are basic anchor points of living. Many of the troubled people I know have neglected these fundamental aspects of daily life. A lot of moodiness, depression, nervousness, and even craziness improves when these simple needs are met in regular fashion. Erratic uncontrolled lifestyles produce erratic uncontrolled people.

Moreover, you'll find out how hard it is to stick to your schedule. Things will "come up" to interfere with your plans; you'll forget; you'll be too tired to cook or exercise; you won't want to get up on time. You'll feel too regimented, in a rut, bored, turned off at times. Then at other times you'll feel satisfied, self-disciplined, confident, enjoying the exercise, pleased with your own ability to cook or jog, refreshed. However you feel, keep returning to the schedule. Keep building the self-discipline even though your feelings fluctuate. If you fail to stay on schedule one time or one day or more, don't just give up on the whole thing. Bring yourself back to the schedule just as you brought your wandering mind back to the focus of attention in the first exercise.

On the whole an organized life is simpler and more satisfying than a scattered one. And it leaves you a whole lot more time to pursue your personal interests in an energetic fashion. Once the schedule becomes habit, it can be used more flexibly to respond to the varying conditions that life brings you. Yet it continues to provide a stable base for your daily existence. Give it a try.

Exercise III

After you have mastered the first two exercises you might try to keep a special diary for a week or more. Divide each page of the diary in half lengthwise. On the left half of the page write a specific time such as 9:03 A.M., and then write what you were doing at that time. Directly opposite, on the right-hand side, write what you were feeling and thinking at that time. A typical entry might read "8:18 A.M. Behavior: Writing a book manuscript carefully on thin-lined paper. My feet are propped up and my back is leaning against a cushion. Feeling: My throat aches, my forehead feels feverish. I'm thinking about communicating clearly. I'm tired and don't feel like writing."

Try to write about the same amount on both sides of the

divided paper (equal amounts about behavior and feelings), and write at least one page a day. It doesn't matter whether you focus on a single narrow time period (such as 8:00 P.M., 8:30 P.M., 8:45 P.M.) or scatter the time through each day (7:00 A.M., 11:00 A.M., 2:30 P.M., 9:45 P.M., 10:30 P.M.). You may change the times each day if you wish.

Your initial tendency will probably be to write a lot about feelings and thoughts and much less about your behavior. After all, how can behavior be as interesting as thoughts or moods or sensations? Resist this tendency. Begin to notice the rich detail of your daily behavior, your minute-by-minute activities. Brushing your teeth, for example, is a complex process of many separable parts. One purpose of the diary exercise is to get you to examine the long behavior sequences we glibly label with a quick phrase—such as "I went shopping for a valentine card"—and to notice the complex elements of behavior of which they are composed. You may even find some elements that can be done better, with more alertness, than before.

Another purpose of the diary is to help you separate conceptually that which is directly controllable in your daily life (behavior) from that which is not (feelings). See how often you misplace feelings on the behavior side of the page and vice versa.

Yet another purpose is to provide a record of the fluctuations of your feelings over a week or longer. It may seem as though you felt satisfied all last week, or depressed, or excited, but if you faithfully maintained your diary in sufficient detail you will be able to see that your feelings hippity-hopped in various directions, that they faded with time unless you did something to restimulate them, and that they often had little to do with your immediate behavior. The glow of having lunch with a good friend (feeling) may still be warming your psyche as you drive your car out of the restaurant parking lot (behavior). You may, in fact, have trouble identifying any emotional state when you were deeply involved in that video game or the second mile of your morning jogging exercise.

Exercise IV

The next three exercises constitute one set. They involve making a gift, writing a letter, and cleaning up your neighborhood. The next time you feel depressed and unloved make something with your own hands for someone else. The gift can be brownies or macrame or potted clippings from your plants or whatever. The important elements are that you make (not buy) the gift for someone else (not yourself) and that you start on it when you are feeling terrible (not thoughtful and loving).

The second task involves writing a letter to someone you care about when you are feeling abandoned or isolated. The letter should contain nothing at all about your current sad state. It should inquire about the other person's activities, it should mention your gratitude for specific things that person has done for you, and it should contain an apology for specific things you have done or failed to do in keeping the relationship close. If you have moved to a distant city and are regretting the paucity of letters from old friends, you might write asking them about the latest news, recalling good times together, thanking them for helping you pack, and apologizing for not sending the business brochures they asked you to pick up in your new city, and so forth. If you haven't moved but feel distant anyway, a valentine (even in September) to a parent or friend will do the trick.

For the third task, pick a time when you have been sitting around feeling sorry for yourself, grab some big bags, and set out to fill them with litter from your neighborhood. You may wonder what people will think of you wandering around stowing rubbish in your bags. That's fine. Let them think what they want while you help clean your community.

Need I explain the purpose of these exercises? They aim to pull you into constructive, self-sacrificing activity just at the time when your feelings were pulling you into self-centered activity. See what happens to your mood as you get involved in giving yourself away.

Exercise V

For this experience I would like you to spend at least one whole day exploring your purposes. Take a mental step backward from your behavior and get both closeup and panoramic views of your aims. (There are long-range and immediate purposes.) Throughout the day keep asking yourself "What is my purpose in doing this now?" Then answer that question for yourself. What is my purpose in brushing my teeth now? What is my purpose in making this telephone call that I'm dialing now? What is my purpose in lifting this spoonful of ice cream to my lips now? What is the purpose of my attending school at this time? What is my purpose in asking my purpose?

These questions call for specific replies, personal replies, current replies. Of course, there are no wrong answers to these questions. There are dishonest answers, though. If you catch yourself lying to yourself about your purposes simply ask yourself about your present purpose in lying to yourself, too.

Everyone needs direction in life. Drifting about aimlessly produces even less satisfaction than living in order to hurt or destroy. There is no accomplishment when there is no purpose by which to measure success or failure.

You may have noticed that Exercise III, the diary exercise, was an attempt to get you to examine feelings and behavior just as this exercise prompts you to examine purpose. With this meditative effort we have completed one stage of examination of the feeling/purpose/behavior triad of Constructive Living.

Exercise VI

This exercise gives you practice in noticing your surroundings. One of the key aims of Constructive Living is to pull your attention away from excessive self-focus and push it outward until you begin to see your self as part of your own surroundings. That perspective requires a lot more attention to our environment than we normally give it.

It is easier to start this exercise by yourself. Take a walk in unfamiliar surroundings. Any place will do: a forest, a park, a shopping center, a residential street, anywhere. Try to take in as much as possible. Memorize the details of this strange environment as if you were going to be examined on it the next day. What are the colors of the tree trunks, drapes in the windows, advertisements? What is the texture of the surface you're walking on? What contrasts do you see? What blending? What flaws? What is artful? How do sounds change as you walk? What subtle odors are present?

Pay attention. Of course, there are details your conscious mind will miss. Do the best you can while ignoring, for the moment, your own responses to this environment. Disregard whether you like or dislike what you experience, whether you feel hungry or bored, random thoughts about tomorrow's plans and yesterday's achievements. Such intrusions may pop into your awareness. When they do simply dismiss them and get back to noticing your surrounding world just as you returned your attention to the object in Exercise I.

The next step is to do the same exercise but this time in a setting with which you're familiar. Again, try to do it with no one else around or only strangers. Note particularly what you never saw before or hadn't noticed in a long time. Go for minute details. If you aren't surprised by the wealth of new sights and smells and touch sensations, you aren't involving yourself sufficiently in the noticing.

Try sketching these familiar surroundings from memory. What did you leave out? Try making a smell map of the area, charting where fragrances arise, fade, and mingle as though on a topographical map. What background sounds have you been ignoring for weeks or years?

The next step is hardest for me and for most other people, too. Try the same exercise at a party or other social gathering. Notice the details of people's names as they are introduced, their clothing and accessories, their fragrances and sounds. Attend to the room decor, the play of lights, the rising and falling of party noises.

What makes this last part of the exercise so hard is that a social get-together requires our participation. We aren't permitted merely to stand back and observe. We have the responsibility (and pleasure) of joining in. So we must slip in and out of this meditative state as the social circumstances require. Perhaps this attentiveness to the environs can occur only a few seconds at a time before we are pulled back into a conversation. That's sufficient. To know experientially (not merely intellectually) that such a perspective is possible in these surroundings, too, becomes the important insight here.

When I have my clients close their eyes and quiz them about the color of the rug in my office, when I ask them to report on a new route they traveled as a passenger in someone else's car, when I ask them the position of their slippers when they woke up this morning, I am asking questions about the focus of their attention. If it hasn't been turned toward these aspects of the environment, where has it been? One can predict rather safely that the more troubled my clients are, the less ready they are to answer these questions—and the more likely they are to have attention focused inward away from the simple reality of their immediate surroundings.

In a way we are like speeding passenger trains rushing through a landscape at sixty miles per hour. Some folks live their whole lives in the dining car or the sleeping berth; some shovel coal day and night to keep their boilers going; some dangle their legs from the tail of the caboose lost in the past; others sit on the cowcatcher trying to predict the next turn of the rails. A few sit on top of the train and get a view of the surrounding landscape. And still fewer transcend the train and landscape to see how the two fit together into a single moving picture.

The more we notice, the more we see what truly needs to be done . . . and the more we act to bring about positive change in our world. That attention and that effort provide the basis for Constructive Living.

Exercise VII

Writing poetry can be a helpful exercise when it leads you to detailed observation of the reality around you. Poetry that focuses only on the ebb and flow of your passions and other internal events is less satisfactory. Even poetry focused on emotions gives you some distancing from your feelings as you seek to describe them artistically. But noticing events and elements of the world around you (the nuances of traffic sounds, the sturdy ants that appear only in the evening, the worn paint on your car's steering wheel, the change in stride made necessary by new boots) and finding the aesthetic and instructive aspects of them shifts your awareness to the reality in which you are immersed.

Japanese haiku and tanka verses are aimed in large part at concisely presenting some aspect of reality the reader will recognize while offering insight or evoking a special feeling associated with it. The following haiku (in translation) illustrate this sharp observation of reality:

> You can see the morning breeze
> Blowing the hairs
> Of the caterpillar.
> Buson

> After the moon-viewing
> My shadow walking home
> Along with me.
> Sodo

Perhaps the most famous haiku of all is Basho's:

> The old pond
> A frog jumps in
> The plop sound.

One cannot write such poetry while being self-focused. The senses must be sharply attuned to sights and sounds and smells and touch to notice the ultimate basis for these creative insights: reality.

Exercise VIII

Where do you usually sit at home when you are down in the dumps? Take that chair and change it somehow so that you won't sit on it. Put tape across the arms, put tacks on the cushion, turn it upside down. I don't want you to head automatically for that chair and sit down.

If you are having trouble sleeping, you may want to do the same with all your chairs at home for a while. Get through an entire evening or weekend without once sitting down at home. Watch television standing up or exercising. Go out. Eat standing up. Read with the book propped on your fireplace mantle or some other high place. Fall into bed physically tired, and see how your sleep is affected.

These suggestions help you to break the habit pattern of just sitting around. Physical activity, movement of your body, is helpful in keeping your spirits up. Rather than sitting while trying to decide what to do next, start doing something constructive. Anything at all. If there is a task that is more important for you to be doing at that time, it will pop into your awareness as you work.

Put notes about your purposes on the refrigerator, on the bathroom mirror, in your car, and elsewhere. They will be reminders of your new resolution to live purposefully.

Remind yourself in other ways through rearranging furniture, dressing differently, changing your hairstyle, and so forth. The tendency to slip back into old, undesirable behavior patterns must be overcome by constant alertness and recharging of purpose. Changes in your dress and food and environment and reading material will keep you aware that you're working toward a constructive lifestyle. It's fine to have energy and sensitivity, but don't retreat from the world because of a misdirection of these qualities. Redirect them to challenge life. You don't *need* confidence!

The same sensitivity that caused you to notice your own faults, mistakes, and weakness can be directed toward noticing others' needs and helping them feel at ease. The energy that was directed at protecting yourself and avoiding risk can be rechanneled toward giving yourself to others and meeting head-on the demands of whatever reality brings you.

Playing the shy oyster or timid ostrich just doesn't pay off consistently in life. You *know* that. Neither does the role of heedless charging water buffalo. The key to successful living is to pay attention and act purposefully. Life won't be trouble free that way—but then no life is trouble free. Being on top of the world depends upon being *on top of* the world: being in control of you acting in the world.

Maxims

1. *Run to the edge of the cliff and stop on a dime.*
There are three key words here: run, edge, stop. When confronted by a problem in life, do what can be done to solve it (run); use every recourse in moving to the moment of solution (edge); and remain unattached to the outcome (stop). The goal is wholehearted commitment to the *doing,* not to the result. If we merely meander toward the solution, or if we try only one recourse when several are possible, or if we rely on "everything working out well," there will inevitably be discontent because problems do not consistently resolve themselves as we want.

2. *Don't put your life on hold.*
While waiting to learn the results of some action (college admission, job interview, bar exam) or anticipating some event (a birthday, a wedding, a vacation) there may be a tendency to simply get through the hours or days. Life lived without awareness not only dissipates the time but promotes the habit of slothful inattention.

3. *All I can do is . . . the next thing and the next thing and the next.*
Moment by moment, reality brings us tasks in just this order.

4. *Have it be the way it is.*
    Variant: *Things turn out the way they do.*
    Variant: *It's not the way it ought to be; it is the way it is.*

Accept reality as it is. Then, if necessary, act to change your circumstances.

5. *Stick it in your* hara.
The *hara* is in the lower abdomen. It is considered by the Japanese to be the center of spiritual energy. This maxim is offered to people who act impulsively without considering the effects of their words. They are advised to put their thoughts and feelings into their *hara* and wait. When they have ripened or faded away, then it is time to act.

6. *What needs to be done next?*
   Variants: *Hmmmm, what needs to be done next?*
   That's interesting; what needs to be done next?
   I'm feeling _____; what needs doing now?
   That's reality; what needs to be done now?
Rather than fixing on some feeling or circumstance we are simply to note its existence and move on to what reality has brought for us to do.

7. *Keep on doing what needs to be done.*
This is perhaps the most frequently used Moritist maxim. It is positive, active, purposeful.

8. *Symptoms are misattention.*
Psychological symptoms come into existence when they invade awareness and interfere with our doing what needs doing. When attention is refocused on constructive activity, symptoms disappear.

9. *Give and give until you wave goodbye.*
In some relationships (the principle applies to jobs, as well) there is psychological disengagement long before the breakup. We recommend that both members give themselves to the rela-

tionship right up to the moment of separation. Sometimes the separation becomes unnecessary when this effort is put forth, but in any case there is no regret for something left undone. We aim at doing everything well until we begin something else. Then we do that well, too.

10. *Quit only when you're succeeding.*
When a job is boring or difficult the person in a neurotic moment is likely to want to quit. This maxim advises us to stick through the initial discomfort and to resign if that becomes necessary only after mastering the job (adjusting to the prostheses, making a go of the marriage, adapting to the new community). To change after success rather than after failure gives a different psychological tone to subsequent activities such as jobseeking. Above all we want to avoid building a history of failure.

11. *Many "me's."*
     Variant: *Changeable people.*
We change continuously. We all have multiple identities. One need not buy the mistaken notion that a person is "neurotic" or "weak" or "a failure" or "hard to live with." We aren't fixed rigidly into a particular character. For simplicity we write about neurotic people, but it is merely shorthand for people in neurotic moments.

12. *Every moment a fresh one.*
What I did just now is already past. Whether that moment brought success or failure the next moment is now arriving. Herein lies existential hope—not as a feeling, but as an integral part of reality.

13. *Unpleasant doesn't mean bad.*
     Variants: *Pain brings us to the present.*
     Anxiety breeds caution and preparation.

Worry provokes planning.
Suffering got us here.

These maxims all point to the possibility of good in even the most unpleasant feelings. The goal in Constructive Living is not to eliminate these feelings, but to accept and even use them as signs of what needs to be done.

14. *Emergency? Watch what emerges.*
Even when action must be immediate there is time to notice what needs to be done.

15. *Action brings experience; experiential knowledge is dependable.*
People in neurotic moments tend to overplan and underact. Our imagination creates unreal dilemmas as well as likely scenarios. We often try to understand with the intellect what can only be tested through behavior. Action cuts through fiction by producing reality-based experience.

16. *Exchange yourself for another.*
     Variants: *Go be a wave.*
     Melt into the moment.
Self-consciousness disappears when attention is merged with reality. When the shy woman loses herself in her companion, when the beachgoer becomes the wave in which he swims, there is no awkward introspection.

17. *Moldy perfume.*
     Variants: *Suffering grows from a seed of beauty.*
     Muck grows out of the lotus.
     Look for the beautiful source.
Every painful symptom emerges from a positive desire. The terrified public speaker wants to do well. The hypochondriac wants good health and a long life. When the proper goals are lost from

sight, when attention is misdirected, when improper means are employed, then symptoms appear. We must discover the positive purposes underlying our symptoms.

18. *Active rest.*
Rest can often be achieved by turning from one sort of task to another. Lying down can be a task worthy of attention, too, but some people try to use long periods of rest as escape from dealing squarely with their problems. Others, who suffer from neurotic insomnia, are advised to refrain from naps during the day and to refresh themselves through active rest. With very rare exceptions the body assures itself sufficient sleep.

19. *Self-centeredness is suffering.*
Selfish, self-protective, self-serving attitudes always produce neurotic suffering. Self-abandonment in the service of a positive goal always reduces neurotic suffering. Ordinary suffering is unavoidable, but self-focused suffering is unnecessary. Buddhists call it "suffering on top of suffering."

20. *I wish I weren't miserable.*
Misery is often associated with wishful statements beginning "I wish . . ." or "If only . . ." or "They ought to . . ." or "He should have . . ." or "Why didn't I . . ." and so forth. When we're miserable, we're miserable. Now what needs doing next?

21. *Two kinds of "can't."*
In neurotic moments we may use the words "I can't" to mean something other than "it is, in reality, impossible for me to do." We sometimes use "I can't" to mean "I won't" or "I didn't in the past" or "I'm afraid to." In the latter case we may forget which sort of "I can't" we used and wrongly convince ourselves of an action's impossibility. Only the first kind of "can't" is allowed in Constructive Living.

22. *Depressed? Get moving!*
Physical activity is important in most neurotic conditions. Feel like it or not, activity is a basic means of influencing emotions indirectly.

23. *Flounder with full attention.*
Failure provides a new set of circumstances, a fresh moment, and always something that needs to be done. Don't miss the opportunity to notice what needs doing whether you just succeeded or failed.

24. *Confidence follows success.*
Some people believe they should undertake a venture only after they feel confident of their ability to do it. With that attitude they rarely start any ventures. Trembling and unsure, without confidence, we give life a try. Confidence comes *after* we have succeeded, not before.

25. *You care about what you care for.*
By taking care of something, physically caring for it, a genuine interest and affection for it may be developed. Love is not only demonstrated by actions; it is developed by them.

26. *Freedom through discipline.*
We never know the materials and techniques of a craft until we discipline ourselves to study and practice it. Then, with increasing mastery, comes the possibility of improvisation. Life is not conducted freely or well when we have no mastery over our behavior.

27. *There is always just enough time to do what needs to be done.*
Why rush? What needs doing in this moment can only be done in this moment. Then comes another moment.

28. *Feelings are for feeling.*
Feelings aren't for explaining, for justifying, or for acting out. They are to be noticed, experienced, and accepted while we go about doing what needs doing.

29. *When you're not noticing your grief, where is it?*
Some people would argue that grief, or any other emotion, is stored chemically in the body even when we're not aware of it. That's like saying that the mind and the brain are the same thing. They're not. Consciousness is only consciousness; it may be influenced by the physical world, but it is never identical to it.

30. *You can't make anyone else feel good.*
If you can't control your own feelings, how can you control the feelings of anyone else?

*31. *Feelings change like the Japanese sky.*
Emotions are sometimes cloudy, sometimes sunny. Who can control the weather?

*32. *If it's raining and you have an umbrella, use it.*
Don't endure unpleasant circumstances that can be changed by action.

*33. *Don't try to shovel away your shadow.*
Don't try the impossible task of trying to control your feelings by willpower.

34. *Watch out for the waves!*
Like the surf, the waves of reality keep on coming at us. If we're knocked down by one we must look quickly for the next in order to avoid being knocked down again.

*Morita's words in translation.

35. *Making friends with fear.*

Struggling with feelings such as fear as though they were adversaries merely intensifies their effects. Recognizing them as old acquaintances, even treasuring them, allows them to fade in time without stimulating a new struggle.

36. *Behavior wags the tail of feelings.*

Behavior can be used sensibly to produce an indirect influence on feelings. Sitting in your bathrobe doesn't often stimulate the desire to play tennis. Putting on tennis shoes and going to the courts, racket in hand, might.

Afterword

I'M SITTING at a desk with an arrangement of orchids and the strange protea blossoms that look like they came from the sea rather than the slopes of Haleakala. It has rained most of the day here in Wailuku. The clouds seem to tumble out of the Iao Valley and pour all over sky and earth. Is there a storm factory up the valley? Another rainy season on Maui.

The Health Center Pacific is a beautifully furnished office facility in Wailuku, all whites and deep browns with plants and *sumi-e* scrolls everywhere you turn. And a hanging sign of wood-framed smoked glass that would make a perfect coffee table if legs were added. I've come here to do Morita Therapy and other Japanese "quiet therapies." How in the world did I end up here?

There are a lot of enigmas in my life—an anthropologist better known by psychologists in this country, an American with more of a reputation in Japan than at home, a Christian doing Buddhist-based therapies. Perhaps it's not so unusual, after all, to find myself so far in miles and temperature from my icy Ohio birthplace on this February afternoon. The key to this paradox is Morita Therapy, how I stumbled upon it, and how it insinuated itself into my life, both professional and private. Perhaps the tale is worth telling—if only to demonstrate the unpredictability of human existence.

Upon enlisting in the U.S. Navy I knew next to nothing of Japan; of course, I had never heard of Morita Therapy. The instructors at Radioman School in San Diego promised the top students their choice of duty stations. I worked hard with an eye toward shore duty in England. The sea never did agree with me. In the end my duty assignment turned out to be a ship in the Pacific—so much for navy promises! By such an unforeseen and unwelcomed circumstance a life course was changed. For the attack transport *U.S.S. Navarro* took me, queasy yet curious, to Japan.

I was eager to get off the ship when we docked at Yokosuka, Kobe, and Nagasaki. In particular, my fancy was caught by the austere black ink paintings called *sumi-e.* Shopkeepers patiently puzzled through my hodgepodge of drawings, hand signals, broken Japanese, and English to direct me to shops with unintelligible signs but scrolls of immeasurable beauty.

What struck me was the combination of Japanese courtesy yet a sense of distance, a sort of psychological space separating us. I sensed a holding back, a censoring of speech and facial expression among these Japanese. It appeared to be sort of self-control that was as automatic and natural as it was all-embracing. Stranger still, as I became aware of this Japanese reticence to reveal the self it also became clear that I myself shared this quality. For all my American show of openness I found myself reluctant to disclose to others anything but the face that would keep our relationship harmonious and free of conflict. Perhaps if I could understand the "inscrutable" Japanese mind, I would have a better handle on my own. Thus began my fascination with the Japanese psyche. Over the years I've come to realize that we humans are much more alike than we are different. But our superficial differences do stand out and thus are valuable in attracting attention and exploration. They are individual entrances to conceptual caverns of human psychology large enough to hold us all.

My navy tour completed, I entered UCLA with the naive purpose of understanding the Japanese mind. Since the courses in psychology seemed rather narrow and specialized for this goal, I gradually shifted to a broader discipline: anthropology. The new freedom suited my tastes. I wanted to know *everything* about Japan. It took time to learn that a holistic perspective is different from mastering all there is to know about a subject.

I bought many books on Japan. Just knowing that they were on the shelf gave me foolish reassurance. But most of them had bibliographies with titles I didn't possess. The impossibility of the exponential task of merely reading the literature on the Japanese people gradually dawned on me. Moreover, the writing in English about the workings of the Japanese mind seemed— what shall I say?—"exterior" somehow, as if the author were guessing or simply presenting hypotheses based on general principles. I sought a more intimate acquaintance.

The writings of Morita therapists in English seemed to have that quality of intimacy. These Japanese authors wrote as if they had listened seriously to troubled people (much as Elisabeth Kubler-Ross listens to dying people) and had thought hard before putting pen to paper. They presented journals: first-person accounts of suffering and cure. What they wrote about the Japanese often checked out with my own experience from this quite different culture.

When a Morita therapist, Dr. Kenshiro Ohara, came to the Los Angeles Suicide Prevention Center for study, a perfect opportunity presented itself for further investigation of Morita's ideas. I was invited by the center to interpret for him and to collaborate on the translation of several of his papers on suicide. Our friendship grew. When Dr. Ohara returned to Japan I followed in order to begin fieldwork for my dissertation on Morita Therapy.

There's a certain anxiety involved in living in another culture, particularly when one has the innocent ideals I had. I expected to be competent; yet I couldn't read many of the shop signs or notices I received in the mail, I didn't know how to pay an electric bill, the jingling melody I heard outside was not the expected ice cream wagon but a garbage truck, the foods in the markets were alien, the bank demanded an ink seal alongside my signature, and I kept passing out on crowded commuter trains from heat and weakness generated by a rebellious intestinal tract.

Furthermore, I kept making behavioral mistakes. Probably they were viewed by the Japanese as the everyday mistakes one might expect from a foreigner. But my perfectionism obliged me to respond to any small error with embarrassment. I felt that I was a Representative of American Anthropology to these people and carried a grave responsibility in that role. It all appears silly and grandiose as I look back, but perspective was lacking at the time.

Moreover, social relationships were deteriorating because of my reticence to reveal my faults to others. For one thing, I pretended to know more of the Japanese language than I did. It was awkward to continually interrupt interviews with "Please say that again" or "Please speak more slowly" or "I didn't understand what you said." Pulling out a dictionary to look up word after word certainly made *me* feel uncomfortable; I can only guess what it did to my companion's flow of thought. I began nodding and smiling even when missing whole sentences. It sounds rather harsh to put it this way, but I lied about my competence in the language through my behavior.

One result was that interactions became complicated. I couldn't talk with a Japanese for too long or my lie might be discovered. I couldn't talk with the same person too often for fear there would be a reference to something previously said. Again, my incompetence would be revealed. My main concern was to present a fine image instead of reality.

All this time I was studying a therapy that advised accepting feelings as they are and getting on about doing what really needs doing. Eventually, the possibility dawned on me of applying these principles to my own case. It was necessary to accept my embarrassment, my hesitancy to reveal my faults to others, and get on with the business of the interviews and observations. There was no sudden breakthrough, but the research began to progress once I got these priorities straight. I worked less on trying to control my feelings, less on trying to impress others, and more on the study I had come to do. To write about it is simple, but the process required a lot of attention, moment by moment, to the immediate tasks at hand.

Wisely, the Morita therapists required me to undergo treatment as a patient and to treat other patients as therapist in addition to my role as outside observer. They weren't aiming at converting me from anthropologist to psychotherapist. Rather, they have a sensible distrust of an outsider's intellectual understanding of what they do. Today, as I read recent articles written in English by people who have only visited a few clinics in Japan or read about them in the literature, I can understand the Moritists' caution. Some of them saw me then as the person who would introduce their therapy to the Western world. They wanted to be sure I had *experiential* knowledge of it.

The dissertation was completed in 1969 and *Morita Psychotherapy,* the book which grew from it, appeared in 1976. In the meantime we were developing a truly American Morita Therapy. I was training psychiatry residents and clinical psychology interns at the USC School of Medicine. Workshops for social workers, health professionals, and volunteers were held. Articles and chapters began appearing in books. We were careful to avoid a trendy Southern California image. Instead we emphasized the solid fifty-year history of Morita Therapy in Japan.

By the end of 1981 a small corps of Americans had been certified in the practice of Morita guidance. Those certified at the TōDō Institute in Los Angeles and at the Health Center Pacific on Maui had demonstrated not only a working knowledge of the principles. They had also shown the ability to apply the principles in their own lives and in the lives of their patients as they practiced under my supervision.

Sitting here at the Health Center Pacific in Maui where I've come in order to train a few more health professionals, it is satisfying to see that Morita's ideas are no longer confined to Japan. Western ideas have been incorporated into an international Moritist theory, and American innovations have changed the Japanese theory and practice. There is a rich exchange as our articles in English are translated and published in Japanese to stimulate new perspectives and practice there.

At present the West has nothing to match the Moritist hospitals and clinics or the five-thousand-member Moritist organization, Seikatsu no Hakkenkai. But in this volume and its earlier companion, *The Quiet Therapies,* I have tried to show the practical applicability of Morita's ideas within a Western context. In the end, I haven't learned about them and us . . . only about Us.

Selected Readings

Brandon, David. *Zen in the Art of Helping.* New York: Dell, 1976.

Carkhuff, Robert. *The Art of Helping.* Amherst, Mass.: Human Resource Development Press, 1973.

Carrington, Patricia. *Freedom in Meditation.* New York: Anchor Doubleday, 1978.

Frankl, Viktor. *Man's Search for Meaning.* Boston: Beacon, 1968.

Herrigel, Eugen. *Zen in the Art of Archery.* New York: Random House, 1971.

Kapleau, Philip. *The Three Pillars of Zen.* Boston: Beacon, 1965.

Kopp, Sheldon. *If You Meet the Buddha on the Road, Kill Him!* New York: Bantam, 1972.

_____. *An End to Innocence.* New York: Macmillan, 1978.

Kora, T., and Ohara, K. "Morita Therapy." *Psychology Today,* October 1973.

Perls, Frederick. *Gestalt Therapy Verbatim.* Lafayette, Calif.: Real People Press, 1969.

Reynolds, David. *Morita Psychotherapy.* Berkeley: University of California Press, 1976.

_____. *The Quiet Therapies.* Honolulu: University Press of Hawaii, 1980.

_____. "Morita Therapy." In R. Corsini (ed.), *Handbook of Innovative Psychotherapies.* New York: Wiley, 1981.

_____. "Naikan Therapy." In R. Corsini (ed.), *Handbook of Innovative Psychotherapies.* New York: Wiley, 1981.

_____. "Psychocultural Perspectives on Death." In P. Ahmed (ed.), *Living and Dying with Cancer.* New York: Elsevier, 1981.

_____. *Naikan Psychotherapy.* Chicago: University of Chicago Press, 1983.

Reynolds, David, and Farberow, Norman. *Suicide: Inside and Out.* Berkeley: University of California Press, 1976.

Strauss, Anselm. *Chronic Illness and the Quality of Life.* St. Louis: Mosby, 1975.

Wienpahl, Paul. *Zen Diary.* New York: Harper & Row, 1970.

HAWAII Production Notes

This book was designed by Roger Eggers.
Composition and paging were done on the
Quadex Composing System and typesetting
on the Compugraphic 8400 by the design and
production staff of University of Hawaii
Press.

The text typeface is Garamond and the display typeface is Compugraphic Americana.

Offset presswork and binding were done by
Vail Ballou Press, Inc. Text paper is Glatfelter
Offset Vellum, basis 50.